My Line of Life

W. Heath Robinson

PREFACE

This is a new edition of My Line of Life, the William Heath Robinson autobiography, which had been out of print for many decades. First printed in hardback by Blackie in 1938, the autobiography captures the spirit of the artist and reflects the opinions of the time.
The reprinting of the book has been paid for by the generosity of the Friends of the Heath Robinson Museum who wanted to mark the 150 th anniversary of William Heath Robinson's birth (May 2022). We hope re-issuing his book will bring the artist alive to a new generation.

Ruth McNeil, chair of the Friends of the Heath Robinson Museum.

Acknowledgement

Our thanks to those who donated so generously to the Friends' Fund Raising Appeal, Summer 2021, and for making this reprinted edition of My Line of Life possible.

Geraldine Beare
Mrs Verena Dorothy Bray
Ms Pat Clarke
Mrs Jill Cock
Cathy Elliott
John and Nicola Greenwood
Gryphon Educational Trust
Ms Karin Heath
Mrs Ann Kopka
Ruth and Ian McNeil
Prof Anthony Pinching and Katherine Pinching
Mr Peter Polkinghorne
The Prentice Family Trust
Mr Crispian Strachan
The Tansy Trust
Mrs Cynthia Wells

W. Heath Robinson

My Line Of Life

Third edition 2022

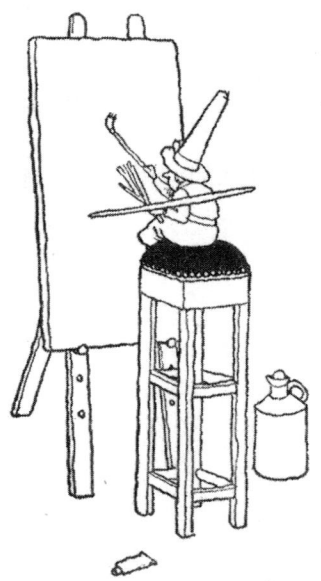

ISBN 978-1-3999-1218-1

heathrobinsonmuseum.org

First published by Blackie & Son Ltd. In 1938

Printed and bound in Great Britain by
Print2Demand Limited
Westoning and Ashford

To
My Daughter
JOAN

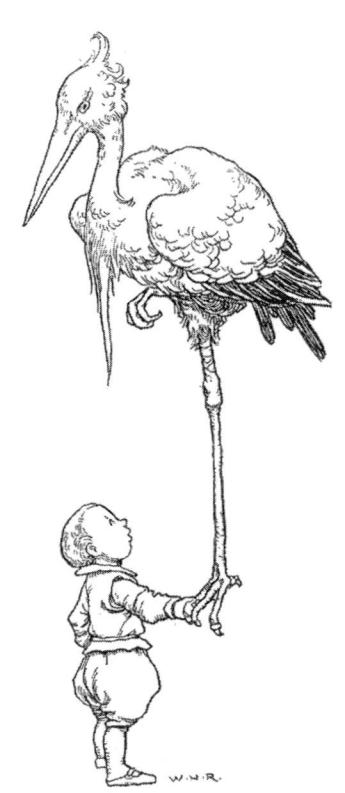

CONTENTS

Chap.		Page
I.	Grandfathers	1
II.	London N.	11
III.	Tom's Castle	23
IV.	School	35
V.	Holidays	49
VI.	Friends and a Funeral	61
VII.	Art Students	69
VIII.	The Landscape Painter	79
IX.	Bread and Butter	89
X.	Uncle Lubin	101
XI.	Big Business	117
XII.	Pinner	131
XIII.	War	143
XIV.	In the Country	159
XV.	The Business Man	169
XVI.	Ordinary People	187
	Index	197

LIST OF PLATES

	Facing Page
W. Heath Robinson at the present day — — Frontispiece	
My Great-Grandfather Heath — — — — —	4
Those chilly mornings: ingenious devices fitted in the most up-to-date flats and maisonettes in Golders Green — — —	92
An Illustration to " Rabelais " — — — — —	96
Spring cleaning in Highgate Woods — — — —	110
Myself and my " double " (played by Mr. René Koval) — —	114
Flat Life: the Spare Bedroom — — — — —	136
The button magnets: used by the Germans to render our troops uncomfortable before an attack in force — — — —	146
The subzeppmarinellin for making sure of your enemy — —	150
American barb trousers: for enabling troops to extricate themselves from wire entanglements — — — — — —	152
A protected mine-finder sounding for mines — — —	154
The blow-bomb: an engine for blowing out the fuses of zeppelin bombs — — — — — — — — —	156
The new mortar for bridging chasms — — — —	164
A patent double-action grinder for mashing asbestos fibre —	176
Efficient plant for the successful mixing of treated asbestos fibre with cement — — — — — — — — —	178
W. Heath Robinson: a recent portrait — — — —	194

CHAPTER ONE

Grandfathers

IT is interesting to notice the success with which writers such as W. S. Gilbert, Rudyard Kipling and many others, have illustrated their own works; some with little or no training in drawing. The lack of this, instead of being a hindrance, seems even to have imparted to their illustrations an unsophisticated charm that would otherwise have been wanting. Not often have artists written to their drawings so successfully. I do not, of course, refer to those geniuses who are, at the same time, both artists and authors. There is something amusing in the thought of an artist writing a book, an author making a drawing, or, say, a flautist painting a picture. In such changes of rôle we are too intrigued to be critical. We take a kindly view, and make allowances for weaknesses, due to the use of a foreign medium, which elsewhere we should not pass over so lightly.

I am hoping for such generous consideration of this work of mine. All the more necessary is this to me, as my story is a plain one. Without the help of stirring adventures I embark upon the delicate task of interesting my readers in homely things.

To begin my plain story at the beginning, I was born on the 31st May, 1872, in the suburb of Hornsey Rise in the North of London. Although this was not within the sound of Bow Bells, except perhaps on a very quiet day, I am not far wrong in calling myself a Cockney. My father, who was also born in North London, but nearer to the sound of Bow Bells, was one of a family of artists and craftsmen. Some of these, though unknown to the present generation, did excellent work according to the standards of their day.

My grandfather, Thomas Robinson, the patriarch of the family, started life as a bookbinder in his native town of Newcastle-on-Tyne. In this capacity he bound books for Thomas Bewick, the wood engraver. It is pleasing to think that he may have bound some of those precious first editions of the works of the famous artist and craftsman. He also bound books for George Stephenson, the father of the locomotive, and knew him personally. Eventually, precisely when I do not know, he came up to London to seek his fortune, and travelled from Newcastle in a collier, probably working his passage.

In London he abandoned bookbinding and became a wood engraver. He engraved drawings by Sir John Gilbert, Du Maurier, Charles Green, Fred Walker and other famous artists, for such journals as *The London Journal* and *Good Words*. I do not know where or when he acquired his skill, but specimens of his work display an expert knowledge of his craft, and, what is so necessary for a wood engraver, an artist's appreciation of the drawings he engraved.

He had two brothers, Matthew and Jonathan. I know little more of Great-Uncle Jonathan than that he emigrated to America many years before his grand-nephews were born. Perhaps he fathered that daredevil hatter with the six-shooter, mentioned in a later chapter.

But there was romance for us in the very thought of Great-Uncle Matthew. He was the sailor of the family, and was drowned at sea long before we could have known him. This was unfortunate because he was just the sort of man we should have liked to know. We pictured him as an English Sindbad, enthralling us with tales of his voyages, or by his songs; for we were told that he had a glorious voice. We were also told that he was a tall, handsome man with curling hair; that he was bluff, hearty, brown and breezy as any self-respecting sailor should be. We readily believed all these things, and that his arms were tattooed all over with strange devices.

My grand-father Robinson engraving
(*After a sketch by my uncle, Charles Robinson*)

We rather enjoyed being saddened by the tragic story of his end, which happened in this way. He was one day sleeping in the forechains of his ship—a hazardous thing to do, no doubt, but sailors are like that—when one of his mates, to awaken him, threw a bucket of water over him. The sudden shock of this caused him to lose his balance, and he fell from his precarious couch into the sea. Efforts to rescue him were of no avail and he was seen no more. I still possess two antique Chinese statuettes brought home from one of his voyages. There was something of truth, after all, in the story of Great-Uncle Matthew with the glorious voice, who sailed the seas so long ago.

Unfortunately, my ancestral records do not go back very far. The most remote ancestor of whom I can write with any certainty was my great-grandfather on my mother's side. He started life as an employee on an estate in Lincolnshire. Later we find him keeping an inn in the county of Middlesex, attracted nearer and nearer to London with the rest of the progenitors of the great family Heath Robinson, until London went out to meet them.

There is a legend in the family of an even more remote connexion who

My Great-grandfather Heath
After an old photograph

was convicted of stealing a sheep, and, as we chose to describe it, was suspended from further activities. But, we tried to persuade ourselves, he may not have known that the sheep did not belong to him, and one sheep is much like another. If this argument was put to the judge, he does not seem to have been swayed by it. So long ago was this incident that we children were convinced that the case was tried before Judge Jeffreys.

My grandfather, William Heath, likewise discovered an aptitude for country inn-keeping. He kept three or four at different times. Most of them are still in existence, though not all as country inns. How proud was I in passing one of these recently in Hammersmith. The house was undergoing repairs. The advertising boards and signs had been removed, exposing the old brickwork. Across the front of the building, in large and faded letters, the name of William Heath was disclosed for the first time for well over half a century. This was painted up when the house was still a coaching inn and Hammersmith little more than a country village. There was only one thing to do, and the time of day being in my favour, I did it.

Later I shall have more to relate of my forebears, but enough has been said already to give some idea of the genesis of the family Heath Robinson. My own generation lived at least in reasonable comfort, though not luxuriously. I suspect, however, that we were always living to the top of my father's income. In spite of the precariousness of this, the family budget was so nicely balanced that the younger members never realized how close to the door was the wolf. Fortune was kind, and no calamities overtook us, other than those which in the ordinary course of nature overtake the families of Smith, Brown, Jones and Robinson alike.

My father, another Thomas Robinson, was apprenticed to a watchmaker. Later, following his father, he took to wood engraving. At the time when I first remember him, he had given up this work and become an illustrator.

In his boyhood he longed to be a sailor, as most boys have done at some time, even before the discovery of *Treasure Island*. So strong was this yearning that his mother, who did not at all see eye to eye with him in the matter, took him to the docks. She hoped to discourage him by a nearer and more realistic view of the hardships of a sailor's life than was to be obtained from *Robinson Crusoe* and the tales of Captain Marryat. With this end in view, she interviewed the captain of one of the ships in dock. To her dismay, instead of dissuading the boy, as she fondly hoped, the captain expatiated on the joys of life at sea. He enlarged upon its exciting adventures and the romantic possibilities that are open to the sailor before the mast. The boy was thrilled by the highly coloured recitation.

Suddenly the captain paused and turned to him.

" Do you like sugar?" he asked.

" Yes," replied the boy, thinking that this was perhaps one of the necessary qualifications for candidates. It was, besides, the correct answer.

The captain pursed his lips and shook his head.

" Well, that's a pity," he said. " If there's one thing a sailor must not like, it's sugar. Now just you go home and forget all about it."

The matter was never referred to again, but my father found consolation in making models of ships.

After this he does not appear to have given up altogether his quest for adventure. Among other invitations to disaster, we hear of him, about this time, walking from end to end along the parapet at the top of the old Highgate Archway. I was never told why he did this. I gathered that it was done in the same spirit in which men of to-day climb Mount Everest, more for the glory of the thing than for any useful end that may be served. His mother must have had some anxious moments.

Do you like sugar?

My father worked hard to provide for our little community, which consisted of nine souls, six of whom were children. These included the three musketeers, Tom, the eldest and, in virtue of his years and dominating personality, the leader of the gang; Charles, who had a technique all his own in dealing with our daily problems; and William, about whom all this fuss is being made. Then there were my two sisters, Mary and Florence, and my youngest brother, George, a mere baby, who was regarded with amused tolerance by his elder and more knowing brothers. The family circle was enlarged about this time by the addition of my mother's sister and youngest brother, protégés of my parents. It is true that we had a general servant, a kitchen maid, a nurse, a housemaid and a cook; but as all these retainers were united in one person, our household was not greatly increased thereby.

This useful amalgam of domestic helps was one of those old family servants of whom Peggotty is the type. She had many of Peggotty's good qualities, and like that well-known character she came from Yarmouth. She was not the only faithful servant we had from that town. There must be something in its bracing air that is wholesome and conducive to the

—*My mother, uncle, and aunt. Silhouettes cut by my father*—

raising of devoted servants. Notwithstanding a little dissension now and again, there was friendship between this old servant and my mother, whom I must now attempt to portray.

How shall I describe a good mother? Perhaps in depicting our household, its contentment, the fortitude with which its troubles were borne, and the smooth running of the wheels of our daily life in spite of the occasional roughness of the road, I shall best describe the mother of our family. Quiet in the background, directing, organizing, placating, she was responsible for all of these.

My father's income was mainly derived from his illustrations in the *Penny Illustrated Paper*, the P.I.P., as it was generally called. This was a weekly paper and certainly the pioneer of the Sunday illustrated papers of to-day. It was ably edited by the late John Latey, junior, from the date of its birth almost to the day when it ceased to be. He had an individual style of journalism which he lived to make very popular. He will be remembered and respected by the older frequenters of Fleet Street. His association with my father was one of many years, and each of our families, depending on professional incomes, had similar difficulties to contend with. We had much in common and a friendship which was afterwards to be strengthened by a closer union.

My father's contribution to the *Penny Illustrated* was usually the front-page illustration and that on a double inside page. He was responsible for these features for a great number of years. His work had great journalistic value, and a large public looked for it every week. His subjects included battles, crimes, society functions, earthquakes, and storms and wrecks at sea. These last inspired him most. He was still the boy who wanted to be a sailor. He was extremely conscientious in the attention he paid to correctness of detail, and his drawings were full of animation. How vigorously his British soldier, with one hand grasping the colours of his regiment, hewed his way through the enemy! How criminal was his criminal fleeing from justice; how tragic the scene of the crime, with the little cross to mark where the body was found! What elemental upheavals were his storms!

In those days, before the use of the half-tone block and photographic methods of reproduction, newspapers were invariably illustrated with wood engravings. The news to be illustrated might arrive on the Saturday night, or even on the Sunday morning. It then had to be illustrated, engraved, printed and published by the following Thursday. When the slow process of wood engraving is remembered, this will be admitted to be quick work.

The wood blocks consisted of several rectangular pieces of boxwood, so closely fastened together by a system of screws and bolts that barely a trace of the joins was visible. When the drawing was completed, the engraver would unscrew the pieces and give one to each of his staff to engrave. On the completion of this stage, the pieces would be once more joined together, and the master engraver would engrave over the joins. In this way a large drawing could be engraved in a comparatively short time.

Often have I seen my father at work with the engraver waiting impatiently at his side, ready to seize the block as it was finished and hurry off with it. Sometimes, when there was more hurry than usual, he would take only a portion, leaving my father with a piece shaped like ⌐ or ⌐.

Every Saturday afternoon my father would arrive home with a big black bag, filled with his drawing material and the wood block. Every Sunday morning, without fail, would find him at work at home on his weekly drawing, which had to be finished by the following morning.

There were no photographs to help the illustrator in those days. He had to depend for his material on sketches made by the special correspondent of the newspaper, or on written descriptions. These, however, were very accurate. A portrait drawn by my father from such a description led to the arrest of a famous criminal, Lefroy, the murderer. With what awe we used to examine, with our hands held well behind us, those strange chart-like sketches, covered with written notes and explanations. Perhaps it was a bird's-eye view of a British square, showing the spot where the Arabs broke through, where the stand was made. All this was actually drawn and recorded on the spot.

We always watched keenly the development of my father's drawings, and our interest in the news of the day was thus kept continually alive. Sometimes we made drawings of the same events at his side. We knew all about the campaigns in Afghanistan and the Zulu wars. I could draw a passable Zulu, with feathered headdress, long oval shield and assegai, at an early age. We were deeply stirred by the news of Isandula and of Rorke's Drift, and were grieved at the death of the Prince Imperial. We had, I am afraid, a secret sympathy with that dethroned monarch Cetewayo. Then there was the bad news of Majuba Hill. How we wished we could do something about it! We carefully followed the Egyptian campaign, and hated the Mahdi. We followed in imagination the Khartoum relief expedition, as it progressed stage by stage up the Nile. Finally the news that Khartoum was recaptured and Gordon avenged allowed us to breathe again.

Nor were we lukewarm politicians. A little contemptuous of Dizzy, we liberally tolerated Lord Salisbury, Randolph Churchill, and Joseph Chamberlain, mistaken though they might be in their views. On the other hand we entirely agreed with what Gladstone said in 1884, or whenever he said it. Indeed, we agreed with what he said at any other time, for that matter, and were staunch home-rulers to a boy. The Grand Old Man appealed strongly to our young imaginations. We learnt simple formulæ from our father by which we could draw his portrait. These came in very handy for decorating the margins of our school books and for impressing our friends.

Sometimes on Sunday morning we were taken to see my uncle Charles, who lived not far away. He would be engaged on similar work to my father's, for the *Illustrated London News*. An account of these early days would not be complete without some mention of my uncle Charles. He was my father's only brother and greatest friend. A close companionship united them, only to be ended by my uncle's untimely death. He was an artist of repute in his time, and, though he is not remembered to-day, a reference to the early files of the *Illustrated London News* will prove to the most critical what a great artist he was. Particularly do I remember the series of drawings he made to illustrate the visit of Edward VII, then Prince of Wales, to India, and those he made depicting battles in the Russo-Turkish War.

How many of these Heaths and Robinsons there were! As I try to remember one, others come to view in my mind, asking to be noticed. Although all cannot be recalled in this place, many, I hope, will be mentioned in later pages of this book. None is forgotten; nor is the beneficial influence they have had on my line of life.

CHAPTER TWO

London N.

THE bounds of my daily life as a child, although embracing the whole of my visible world, were confined within narrow limits. Saturday provided almost the only opportunity for exploring these. On that day there was no school, but a welcome lull in the daily routine of the week. Anything might happen on Saturday; it was a day of adventure, an unknown quantity in time. Eagerly anticipated, it so impressed itself on my mind that to this day the close of the week brings something of that old thrill of expectation.

All the other days led up to this, and each was characterized by its nearness to or distance from the end of the week. They had their own individual characteristics too. Monday is still associated in my mind with all that is humdrum and according to routine. I was oppressed by a reaction from the freedom of the week-end. It was a dreary day as a rule. I believe that if weather reports were carefully examined it would be found that Monday was more often rainy than fine.

On Tuesdays the weather seems to have cleared, since, as I remember, it was often windy and bright. This was fortunate, as Tuesday was washing day, and the

Washing Day

linen was drying in the sun and wind on the clothes line in the back garden. This was washing day also for most of the houses in the road. Nearly all the gardens were alive and glorious with flapping banners. Neighbours' pants and petticoats flouted one another unabashed across the garden walls. But it was a muddling sort of day for all that, and the steam from the wash-house seemed to penetrate the lower rooms. All the household linen was washed at home and dried in the garden, and those responsible for these activities let themselves go and made a day of it.

There was not much time to spare for children on washing day. We were always in the way, and the back garden was unplayable because of the clothes props and the wind-blown sheets and under-garments. However, there was one consolation for us; although it was invariably late in coming to the table, we had Irish stew for the midday meal. Perhaps this was a concession to the taste of our Irish washerwoman. Maybe this was her best defence against the ravages to the constitution caused by continually bending over a steaming tub, in a welter of soap suds.

Wednesday and Thursday were just ordinary days, though Thursday was already receiving the glow of the approaching end of the week. After school on Friday, the eve of the great day, we were once more free. Friday night was bath night, and in a tub before the bright kitchen fire we were bathed one by one. Stimulated by this operation, and by a hard rub-down with a warm, sweet-smelling towel, our imaginations glowed with thoughts of what we should do to-morrow. Afterwards, as we supped from our basins of hot soup, we planned great doings, greater than we were likely to achieve. Then, in the snug warmth of our beds, we dreamt of their accomplishment.

Saturday held many delightful possibilities, but the most thrilling of all was a walk along the Great North Road. This was to us a road of enchantment, and the main road of England. It led directly to High Barnet, St. Albans and to York, and finally by roundabout ways to Scotland. These enchanted places could be reached by simply walking straight along the road that passed near our home, if only you were able to keep going long enough. Better still, with Dick Turpin's Black Bess to carry you, the journey to York could be made in one night. English history had marched up and down this road. It had been trodden by armies, rebels, knights, highway robbers; by such well-known travellers as Dick Whittington, Dick Turpin, and not so long before by Oliver Twist and the Artful Dodger. Two or three more young adventurers would now be added to the list.

We started on our pilgrimage soon after breakfast, each with a packet of sandwiches tied with string to his back—and a larger packet of hope. Our nearest objective at that hopeful time in the morning would be High Barnet. There was the church tower at Hadley with its beacon, ready to be lighted at the first sign of the approach of an enemy. We might even get a glimpse of the man on watch, who, we liked to think, was ever ready with match in hand to ignite the fuel at a moment's notice. Then there was a real battlefield to explore, where the battle of Barnet was fought by men in armour. It was fought so long ago that it was not likely that any traces of the fight remained. But you never knew what a careful search would bring to light.

Our journey first took us along the Holloway Road, already busy with beshawled mothers laying in store of meat, vegetables and groceries for the week-end. The tradesmen's carts were being loaded for their Saturday rounds. The errand boys, a wild and irresponsible tribe, were breaking cover, and many other things, as they trundled their barrows along the pavement, whistling shrilly. The "knife-board" buses were carrying the last top-hatted fathers of families to business in town. The driver was chatting cheerily to those fortunate enough to secure seats in front.

Wrapped to the chin in a heavy coat, a grey top hat crowning a blooming countenance, the old London bus driver was a great fellow. He was a true descendant of Tony Weller and inherited Samuel's wit. This, with an occasional flick of his whip, he scattered abroad pretty freely as he journeyed to and from town. We were all proud to claim Charlie as a friend, and to be recognized by him from his seat above the horses. Charlie was the bus driver who knew all there was to know about horses and at whose side my father travelled to town every morning.

Northward bound, we did not allow these scenes of activity to delay us. At this stage, well abreast of one another, my two brothers and I jogged along briskly enough. Lower Holloway and the Nag's Head were soon left behind. We now entered Upper Holloway and passed the old Holloway Hall where bazaars, political meetings and our annual school concerts were held. At the Archway Tavern we diverged from the main road and entered the Archway Road. This was really a cutting through Highgate Hill to avoid the steep rise at this point of the Great North Road, which it joined again farther on.

Dick Whittington had not the advantage of this convenience. Perhaps it was as well, because he was compelled to rest by the milestone on Highgate Hill and listen to the advice of the bells from London Town. Had he been able to follow the easier road, which fortunately did not exist in his day, he and his cat might not have turned again. On the other hand, Dick Turpin, with such help at the beginning of his famous ride, might well have reached York half an hour sooner.

We, however, were not prepared to turn again, at least for a while, and tramped bravely on towards Highgate Archway. This was not the iron bridge you see to-day, but a more romantic structure. It was a tall stone and brick archway, surmounted by three smaller arches, over which passed Hornsey Lane. For us it was the gate to adventure, and as our footsteps, made especially loud for the purpose, echoed through the archway, we felt that we were leaving London definitely behind.

After a short stretch of road that was neither in the country nor out of it, we arrived at the lane that led to Shepherd's Cot. Here the real country began, and we walked a little way along the lane in the hope of seeing the shepherd and his sheep, or at least his cot. Evidently the shepherd had moved, for we saw no sign of them. It was from here that, at a later time, we used to see Baldwin descend by parachute from a balloon, over the grounds of the Alexandra Palace. It will be understood that I refer to the aeronaut, and not to any other illustrious bearer of the name.

Returning once more to our road, we looked across the railway cutting to Highgate Woods, filling the valley and rising to the hills on either hand. Beyond the woods, you could see for miles and miles, a wide expanse of country with village church towers here and there, and the hills far away in the sun. A few steps farther brought us to the Woodman, the first country inn on our route. Here, no doubt, in days gone by the woodman, when tired of chopping trees, came to regale himself. With axe resting at his side, he would tell of all the wonderful things he had seen in the woods. Surely he lived in one of the little cottages close at hand, built almost into the woods. He would only have to open his back door in the early morning and start chopping without waste of time.

Perhaps it was the sight of the inn, or maybe the little parcels on our backs were already becoming tiresome; whatever the cause, the need for refreshment now made itself felt. Although it was as yet quite early in the day, we decided that we could travel more lightly with our food inside us than on our backs. Choosing a suitable place on the grass at the side of the road, we sat down and opened our parcels. After some exchanges—for there was an interesting variety of provisions, we soon finished our meal. Innocently unaware of the misdemeanour it was to become in later years, I am afraid we left the debris at the roadside.

Refreshed, we now trudged on manfully by the Highgate Woods, until the road opened out to fields on either side. The two or three milestones which we passed were of especial interest, but strangely enough they did not seem to succeed one another as rapidly as we had anticipated early in the day. Not so often abreast, we now straggled into Finchley. High Barnet was still a long way off, according to the last milestone, when we arrived at Finchley Cemetery. Here we rested again, wishing that we had not eaten our provisions so early in the morning. Looking wistfully along the road toward High Barnet we realized that we should not reach it to-day. The glamour of our quest remained, but to dispel our disappointment we told ourselves that there was no reason why we should be in such a hurry. High Barnet would always be there. Besides, we all remembered that there were many things we wanted to do at home.

Not admitting defeat, but only postponement of our visit, we started for home. Lacking the incentive with which we had set out, our return was not quite the brisk proceeding it should have been. There seemed to be many side issues to be resolved and to delay our progress. The more weary of our party lagged behind. A few quarrels with other boys, and bickerings amongst ourselves, also delayed us. At long last we arrived home one by one, tired, dusty and hungry.

A good meal which we found awaiting us, and a cold wash over a bowl in the scullery, soon revived our spirits and with them the hope of one day walking to Barnet. Many such attempts were made, sometimes approaching nearer to our goal, sometimes even falling short of Finchley. It was only in later years that we finally succeeded, and then it was something to boast about.

Another of our pilgrimages led us through Finsbury Park, over the Hog's Back beyond, to the village of Hornsey. Our Hog's Back, as I will call it to distinguish it from the hill of the same name in Surrey, was a green down on the farther side of the Park. This hill is now, and has been for many years, covered with rows of suburban villas. We walked through Finsbury Park, a more natural pleasure ground than the Park of to-day. There were no council swings, but, in a grove, some of rustic make hung between the trees.

Our Hog's Back was crossed by a narrow track called Cut-throat Lane. We could never discover how it earned this sinister name, but we felt its evil influence as we walked in dread between the high hedges on either side. Half expecting something gruesome to appear, we were not relieved until the lane brought us to the top of the hill. Here all dread was quickly dispelled by the view before us. We now looked down and across green fields to the old village of Hornsey. In those days, the village seemed from here to be compact and detached from the North of London. It had an old church, of which the tower alone remains to-day, and a country churchyard with fields and cattle beyond. Gray's elegy might well have been written on this spot. There were neat meadows fenced in with white posts, and there were old Georgian houses. As you came over the hill you could hear the cocks crowing in the two or three remaining farmyards of the district.

On fine summer mornings the pleasant sport of butterfly catching, or rather trying to catch them, led us through many country lanes. After climbing Muswell Hill, past tall trees and gardens, we wandered along Colney Hatch Lane, a favourite haunt of whole families of butterflies. Merely regarded as sport, I do not remember that our butterfly catching was remarkable. The butterflies of North London were so swift on the wing. Seeming to enjoy the antics we performed with our nets in our endeavours to catch them, they sported with us rather than we with them. They have all flown long since, and together with the hedges, trees and flower-strewn verges of the lane, are no more.

On Saturday evenings, when days were long, our father and mother would take a walk to the Gate House on Highgate Hill, or farther still along the Hampstead Lane. We looked forward to these excursions of our parents, as each of us in turn would go with them. Though we were glad enough when our turn came round, these walks were rather solemn occasions, as we slowly proceeded in the calm of the evening. At such a time, no doubt, we were more than usually amenable and receptive, and my father could not neglect so favourable an opportunity for moralizing and improving our minds. That he may not always have been successful in this latter aim was certainly no fault of his. At least we were impressed.

We strolled up the old Highgate Hill, whence we could look back upon London, with St. Paul's clearly defined in the evening sun. We came to St. Joseph's Retreat; not the large-domed church of to-day, but a building roofed with dull red tiles, part of which can still be seen. It reminded us of a picture we had seen of a monastery in Switzerland. As stout Protestants, partly brought up on Foxe's *Book of Martyrs*, we looked a little askance at the building as something intrusive and foreign. There was mystery about it too. At its side, Waterlow Park was not the boon it has since become to dwellers in Highgate and Holloway. Ordinary folk like ourselves could only get a peep at Lauderdale House through the gate.

Opposite to the park was the most wonderful house in the whole of Highgate—Oliver Cromwell's house, with a great studded door at its side. It was not difficult to imagine Oliver Cromwell riding out of this, followed by a few Ironsides who had been enjoying the Protector's stern hospitality. Examining the front of the house, we asked ourselves, in which room did he sleep? Where did he have his breakfast? Ireton, his famous general, lived next door—or so we were told. Did they both plan battles over the garden wall at the back of their houses, as we did with our friends at home?

Continuing our walk, we passed old inns and curious little turnings with ancient wooden cottages on either side. At last we reached the top of the hill and the Gate House. The old white gate at its side, we were convinced, was the original gate over which Black Bess had carried Turpin on his way to York. Fortunately, we had no such need for hurry, and, beginning to feel that some refreshment would be welcome, we walked up the steps and entered the inn.

We found ourselves in a long passage hung with paper in imitation of Chinese tiles, on which were to be seen mandarins walking out with their wives beneath weeping willows. On one side of the passage was a small hatch, with a sliding window, let into the wall. As we approached, this was opened from within, giving to our view the smiling face of an old lady, neatly framed by the hatch. She had clearly drawn black eyebrows, with black ringlets on either cheek. Behind her could be seen on shelves squat black bottles of rum shrub and other cordials, each bottle labelled in gold, with the name of its contents in black.

She directed us to the end of the passage, which led into a little square room with bow windows, overlooking the road on two sides. Seated here in comfort, we could see along North Hill many another family group on its Saturday walk. Presently there entered an ancient waiter. He was completely bald except for reddish side-whiskers tinged with grey, and dressed in an old evening suit. Being very aged he stooped a little, and perhaps this was the cause of the many folds in his clothes. He stooped still lower when he asked for our orders. Before giving this, we consulted him as one wise in these matters. After silently considering the situation and taxing his vast experience, he gave us advice which we followed with most satisfactory results.

The Landlady

Sometimes the old lady would come in and chat with us for a little while. I remember wondering how she managed to come from behind the hatch; for she was a very wide lady with spreading black skirts. She used to talk to us of her husband who had died many years before, and showed us an old silhouette of him upon the wall. Bidding her a friendly good-bye, we wended our way home again.

So would end one of those privileged occasions when, in my turn, I would be treated as a single entity and not as one of a group of children. The responsibilities incurred by me as a budding individual would be carefully impressed upon me. Although these walks were so interesting, my parents contrived to give them an air of almost religious solemnity.

It took a long time to dress on Sunday mornings. The clean collars were stiff and difficult to fasten. We were uncomfortable and a little self-conscious in our best suits, as we came down to breakfast. Our dining-sitting parlour was a small basement room a few feet below the level of the road. As we sat at our rather late breakfast, we could already see our neighbours going to church or chapel. Fathers in top-hats, black frock-coats and striped trousers; mothers splendid with parasols and all their Sunday finery; children following, dressed in their best, and each of the party carrying a prayer book and hymn book. Perhaps a disciple of Izaak Walton would pass by, "compleat" with rods, can and jars of bait. He was full of hope and on his way to Hampstead Ponds. Another and rather sinister figure would sometimes cross our vision. He was bending low beneath a large box strapped to his shoulders. We looked at him with aversion, for he was on a cruel errand to snare young birds in Highgate Woods.

We did not often go to church in the mornings. Our mother, who took charge of our religious welfare, only insisted that we should attend one service every Sunday. With the physical happiness of so many to care for, she had no time for religious controversy. Chapel and church were alike to her. That they were places of worship was all that mattered.

To snare young birds in Highgate Woods

Sunday dinner was my mother's crowning feat of the week. In the morning the kitchen was the centre of intense activity. The sirloin of beef would be turning before the fire, suspended from a meat jack. This was a cylindrical brass instrument, fastened to the shelf above the fireplace. Being operated by clockwork, it had to be wound up now and again. The whole of the cooking operations were hidden from view by a zinc-lined cupboard called a meat screen. This was open to the fire at the back, and had shelves upon which the plates and dishes were kept hot. These shelves could be reached through a door in the front of the screen. The potatoes were roasting beneath the joint, and both had to be continually basted with the gravy. There was an oven too, in which a great fruit pie was baking. The work was strenuous, and as the jack ticked regularly in the warm air of the kitchen, the smell of cooking stole gradually through the house, foretelling the delights in store for us.

The stout and ale were supplied from a public house nearby. Without claiming to be superior, we were a little above fetching this ourselves in jugs, as some of the neighbours were not ashamed of doing. Instead, the potman brought it to our door in foaming cans, with a rich smell of fermentation. The empty cans were hung upon the area railings to be taken away by the potman.

We often had a guest to dinner on Sundays. Usually this was a long-nosed young friend, very silent and shy, whom we regarded as a beau of some standing. He had large flowing moustaches which joined short side-whiskers on each cheek. He wore a light suit ornamented with a check of large design, and sported a beautiful tie secured by a brilliant pin.

We never recovered the hymn book

In the evening, my brothers and I went unwillingly to church. The choice of place of worship was left to us, and we had some difficulty in deciding. The three-decker churches were interesting if you went into the highest gallery and looked down at the successive floors below. Rising from the lowest floor of all was the pulpit. We were glad when the sermon came as, if it were not too long, the end of the service was in sight. But the foreshortened view of the clergyman provoked thoughts that would not be restrained. What would happen if some mischievous boy in the gallery were to drop a hassock on his head? Once a hymn book did actually slip from a boy's hand over the balcony and fell upon the heads of the worshippers beneath. We never recovered the hymn book. We knew that we were a nuisance and the old pew-openers knew it too, but we could not help fidgeting. The hassocks would get in the way and the seats would creak. Sometimes the pew-openers would send us away, and we would wander off to some other church.

Sometimes the pew-openers would send us away

"Jack and the Bean-stalk" is a wonderful story. But its most miraculous incident is Jack's discovery, at the top of a mere bean-stalk, of a wide countryside in which was situated the castle of the giant. I felt as Jack must have felt on that occasion, when, one Sunday evening in summer, I mounted with my mother and father the stairs to old Holloway station and stepped upon the platform. Here, to my young eyes, was magic; a wide track of country high up in the sky, of which we had never dreamed in the every-day streets just below. As we waited for our train, a Scottish express roared along this great highway to the wide world beyond.

We were on an excursion to the Alexandra Palace. In those days the Palace was quite in the country, and on Sunday evenings there was a band and the grove was lit up with coloured lights. It was all very romantic; many people promenaded in bright summery costumes around the band and beneath the coloured lamps.

Twilight darkened to night. Then the sleepy homeward journey brought another week of my childhood to a close.

CHAPTER THREE

Tom's Castle

IN the days of which I now write, school does not seem to have played the all-important part in a boy's daily life that it does to-day. This can, at least, be said of the children of parents with small incomes. We were sent of necessity to the best day-school in the neighbourhood, provided that the fees were not too high, and that the school was near enough for the children to walk to and fro twice a day. For the rest, we were left very much to ourselves.

As day-scholars, we spent a large part of our time at home, or with home as the centre of our activities. This freedom was allowed us, not from any lack of interest on the part of our parents, but from a faith in the instinct of children for finding the best way to occupy their time. No doubt this confidence was not always justified, but on the whole it was not misplaced. While every help and encouragement was given, the initiative was always left with us. Without attempting to dogmatize about education, I feel that I owe much to my home life, and little to school. We had to provide our own amusements, and to make many of the things we played with; to the humours of which I was not blind and to which I still respond.

We had to be creative, and to use our imaginations continually and at every turn, to make our crude efforts seem real to us. We had no mechanical models of steamships or trains. I think I may attribute the seeds of inspiration for the humorous drawings which I have since attempted to these early efforts to make things out of homely materials originally intended for some wholly different purpose. In such circumstances drawing became a necessity, and a normal means of expression. My father consistently encouraged it. Our slate stories were an outcome of this. They were told by means of a drawing on a slate, the different stages of the story being presented by gradually modifying the picture, with the aid of sponge and slate pencil. Sometimes they were tales of adventure, of shipwreck, of pirates, of castaways on a desert island and the shifts they were put to. Perhaps the subject would be of a different kind; some great engineering feat, such as building a bridge between two mountains. The bridge would in all likelihood cross a foaming torrent, with full-rigged treasure ships riding on the water. It might be the digging of a coal-mine in the bowels of the earth. They were moving pictures in more than one sense.

Another outlet for any creative skill we possessed was provided by our model theatres. At first we depended upon the materials supplied by the shops, such as those published by Pollock and Remington. A wider field was found for our imaginations when we made our own stage. This was larger and permitted much more ambitious effects than were to be obtained in the ordinary stages bought at shops. The standardized materials we formerly relied upon were of no use to us now. We had to write our own plays, and design our own characters and scenes to fit the new theatre. Our pantomime would take weeks to prepare. There was the lighting with little candles to be arranged. There were trap-doors for the sudden appearance and disappearance of demons and fairies, and many other striking effects. They all had to be tested and rehearsed many times. Our first night was a great occasion, and if our audience was not quite so enthusiastic as we had hoped, we certainly enjoyed it ourselves. We were in the privileged position; we were behind the scenes. The mysteries to be unfolded were no mysteries to us.

No doubt there were many children in those days, and perhaps there are many to-day, who have found and still find amusements in this way. Let us hope so, as it would be difficult to exaggerate the value of the mental exercise involved, or the stimulant provided in this way for a healthy imagination. I must acknowledge the great part they played in my education.

Romance and mystery flourished in this atmosphere. The mystery was not of a psycho-scientific kind. I had never heard of Poltergeists. Ghosts avoided me—that is, as far as I know. They are so intangible that one may walk arm in arm with you along the passage without your knowledge. Although I should have been filled with terror if I had encountered one, I was a little disappointed at this limitation of my experience. I looked for them in the dark corners on my way upstairs at night, and expected one when the candle was blown out and I lay awake in bed. The shy beings seemed as afraid of me as I should have been of them.

Esther our servant, who believed in ghosts, told me that by far the best way to see them was in the company of other people. A good opportunity for this once presented itself to me. A ghost was said to have been seen in the graveyard of the Chapel of Ease in Holloway Road at which Tom, Charles and I made our weekly attempts to become good Christians. One evening Esther took me to see the crowd that assembled every night to witness this visitation. The crowd consisted mostly of women, some carrying children and others resting with their bare arms on the parapet that separated the churchyard from the road. I elbowed my way to the front and peered through the railing surmounting the parapet. I waited long, but the ghost was resting, I supposed, and did not appear that night, so, disappointed I went home to bed. Although I seemed fated never to see a ghost, this was as near as I had ever been to doing so. Later I was to be nearer still when Mr. Bingle's ghost came to our house.

Mr. Bingle was our sweep. He used to visit us periodically, but so early in the morning that we rarely saw him. Only Esther would be up to welcome him. From our bedroom we could hear the rumble and rattle of his brooms and canes in the chimney. One morning he was sweeping the kitchen chimney, when, as we lay awake listening, the noise suddenly ceased and all was very quiet for a little while. Presently we heard Esther running up the stairs in evident haste and knock loudly and insistently at my mother's door. After a short colloquy, we heard our mother and father hurriedly descending the stairs. There was now great commotion below, doors opening and shutting, and people arriving and departing.

Esther

For a little while we bore this patiently and then crept down in our night-shirts. In the panic that reigned, we were hardly noticed. Esther in tears was talking hysterically to a policeman in the passage. From her we learned what had happened.

"I left the sweep to git on with his work in the kitchin while I was layin' the breakfast things in the parlour," she said tearfully.

"Suddenly there was a loud bump and I rushed into the kitchin and there was the poor man lyin' all-of-a-heap on the floor in a dead faint."

All of the family had now collected in the passage, when to my surprise the familiar figure of our family doctor emerged from the kitchen door. He informed my father that the sweep had passed away. He had burst a blood-vessel and died suddenly at his work.

Mrs. Bingle

Mrs. Bingle, who had already been sent for, now arrived. She was not entirely unknown to us. She augmented her husband's income by dealing in old clothes. My mother, whom she addressed as "Dearie", had many mysterious transactions with her at the area door, exchanging well-worn garments for ferns and geraniums. In an Amazonian manner her demeanour to my mother on these occasions was kindly and protective, as to one in a narrower sphere and who knew little of the ways of the world. Mrs. Bingle was an imposing full-bosomed woman in a large be-feathered hat placed high on her dark hair. She wore a white apron over capacious skirts. There was more than a suggestion of Romany ancestry about her tawny skin and deep brown eyes. This was accentuated by her coloured shawl and the silver pendants hanging from her ears. She was in no way perturbed at the prospect of widowhood. She had been married before and no doubt would be again. She now coolly searched her late husband's pockets.

"He sold a horse last night," she told us in explanation of this proceeding.

An old hansom cab occupied by a gentleman in pearlies

After the inquest there was a grand funeral. In recognition of my father's kindly consideration for the Bingles in their difficulties, the procession passed in front of our house. Between our lowered venetian blinds we could see Mrs. Bingle royally seated in a carriage leading the cortege of mourners. The Bingles had a large acquaintance in the coster world. They also knew many horse copers, small tradesmen, and some of the more respectable gipsies. As many as could attend crowded into the curious assortment of vehicles composing the last retinue of Mr. Bingle. Besides the carriages there were several pony carts, one or two four-wheel cabs, some converted tradesmen's vans and at the tail of the procession an old hansom cab occupied by a gentleman in pearlies. Mr. Bingle may not have taken more out of the world than he brought into it but the glories of his worldly state only left him at the edge of the grave.

One night soon after the funeral of Mr. Bingle, my brother Charles awakened us.

"Hush!" said he.

"Can you hear anything?"

We listened intently, and, to our startled imaginations, we seemed to hear the rumble of the sweep's broom in the chimney. In an agony of dread, we all crept close together in one bed. It was only by pulling the coverlet over our ears that we could banish the sound. Eventually it ceased, and we slept. The next morning we confided our terrifying experiences to Esther.

"It was the ghost of Mr. Bingle sure enough," she said, and comforted us with the reflection that we need not have been alarmed, for we could not have seen it even if it had come into the bedroom.

"All sweeps' ghosts is black," she averred.

This was comforting enough in the daytime, but in the dusk we agreed that a black ghost, even if you could not see it, would be more terrifying than a white one.

The next night and the following few nights, we lay awake for hours it seemed, waiting and listening. In course of time, as the sounds did not recur we gradually lost our terrors. We had almost forgotten them when one evening, as we were about to fall asleep, they started again. Once more we sought safety under the bedclothes not daring to leave our beds to seek safety with our parents. Thus we remained until the strange visitation had passed away. In the morning beneath the kitchen chimney was a little heap of brick dust and a dead bird. Thus ended a ghost story without a ghost. It was only revived in our memory, quite unnecessarily, we thought, when the little ragged boys called after us in the streets:

"Who killed the sweep?"

Second sight, mesmerism, ectoplasm and thought-reading were unknown to me; nor did I feel the want of them. I am afraid there must have been something in my mental make-up that checked the visitations experienced by so many people. My father and mother were wisely non-committal about these occult subjects and avoided any discussion about them.

Mystery which was less sophisticated, and with which quite ordinary things and incidents would be imbued, was never far away. A picture on the wall, an illustration in a book, the aspect of a certain room at a particular time of the day, or a dark corner of the staircase would have this elusive quality. An event that was mysterious enough to us, though capable of a simple explanation, would set our fancies at work so convincingly that we would end by believing the stories we evolved.

Although not haunted by ghosts, and quite an ordinary dwelling house of the period, our home, in some unaccountable way, lent itself to these hauntings of the imagination. It was a tall, three-storied, stuccoed house with a basement. The room in which we had our meals and mostly lived was a small parlour on the basement floor in the front of the house. It was a rather dark room, although the basement was only a little below the street level. Behind it were the kitchen and scullery, opening on to the back garden. The lower part of the house was lit by gas—a poor light in those days, and the rest of the house by oil lamps and candles; so that after dark no part of the house was free from the mystery of flickering shadows which electric light has stolen from us.

The narrow passage on the ground floor was, of course, called the Hall. At night it was lit by a gas lamp in an ornamental globe. It was approached by a flight of stone steps leading up to the front door. This floor was only used on Sundays and on ceremonial occasions, and for parties. It was rather grand. Here were the two most important rooms in the house, in which you had to be careful of the furniture and which you only entered attired in your best clothes. These rooms were collectively known as the drawing-room, and were separated by folding doors. We were upon our dignity on the ground floor.

Our bedroom was at the top of the house, and dark and narrow was the staircase up which you hurried at night, candlestick in hand. We slept two in a bed. If we were unable to go to sleep at once, we would hear the noises of the house in the basement far below, a door shutting, or a clatter of plates as supper was prepared for our parents. Then there would be silence, and we would drop off to sleep one by one.

One night I was sleeping with my brother Tom, when we were disturbed by the stealthy opening of the bedroom door. What time it was, there was no means of telling, but it felt like the middle of the night, and as if all in the house, except ourselves and our mysterious visitor, were long since fast asleep. We could see nothing, but presently we heard shuffling footsteps approaching the bed. My brother and I held one another and were too terrified to do more than gasp, " Who's that?" The only reply was an inarticulate growl. After creeping slowly round the bed, the footsteps returned towards the door. We heard them pass out, and the door close.

With the morning our courage returned, but when we talked over our experience with my father no solution of the mystery could be found. Almost without intending to do so, we allowed the incident to develop in our minds. I was surprised to learn that Tom had seen a lantern standing outside the door, with a fierce dog beside it. No doubt, too, our visitor was a tall, dark man with a black visor hiding his face. The more we thought of the affair, the more these details increased, until finally we were proud to be the possessors of such an experience, and of the part we had played.

It happened that on each side of our house, which was one of a row of similar houses, there dwelt a sea captain. Each of these captains had one or more sons, by whom we were proud to be befriended. We all had swings in our gardens, but we, being only the sons of an artist, had the smallest swing of the three. We admitted that this was quite right; the sons of a sailor would naturally want to swing higher. But we could not help being a little envious of the possessor of one of the swings. It was painted green, and had a gilded weather-cock erected above it. Our friends were a little older than we, and had a greater knowledge of the mysteries of life. This they willingly imparted to us in serious talks across the garden wall on summer evenings, in exchange for our milder experiences. Their patronage was welcome to us.

The son of a sea captain was without doubt the right person to whom to confide our nocturnal experience. He would understand. What was marvellous to us was as bread and butter to him. We were not disappointed. The friend whom we consulted was inclined to attribute the whole thing to supernatural influences. He was of opinion, too, that the influences were evil. In support of his argument, he told us of one of his father's adventures. During a terrible storm in which his ship was nearly wrecked, he saw falling from the heavens several balls of fire. In each of these he clearly discerned an angel; but as, his father had assured him, good angels all too rarely appear to man, it was reasonable to suppose that these englobed spirits were evil. It seemed, according to this argument, that our midnight intruder was probably of evil origin; which explanation was sufficiently exciting to be accepted by us as entirely reasonable.

An ever-extending scope for imagination was revealed in the books I now began to read. Discarding nursery tales and fairy stories such as those of the Grimms, Hans Andersen and others, I now began to read boys' books; *Robinson Crusoe*, and tales by such writers as Captain Marryat, Harrison Ainsworth, Fenimore Cooper, Lord Lytton, G. P. R. James and even Sir Walter Scott. I call them "boys' books", though I doubt whether any of these authors professed to write for boys. These were sold in coloured paper covers for the price of fourpence halfpenny. Books would be given to us for birthday presents, after a diplomatic hint as to the one we wanted. Sometimes the money was given to us to make the purchase ourselves.

My brother Tom was a great reader and, as the eldest son, had read more than any of us. His advice, therefore, was considered valuable. Nevertheless, some caution had to be used in accepting this, as very naturally he could not always resist the temptation to advise the purchase of a book which he particularly wanted to read. Choosing a birthday book required care, and it would sometimes be necessary to go into town to get it. The local shops had only a limited selection.

On one birthday I remember searching through Holywell Street, known as Booksellers' Row, with Tom, and with the money for my present held tightly in my pocket. The Row was a delightful place in which to rummage for books. Its narrow way permitted little more than pedestrian traffic, and this was of the quietest character. There was no hurry; it appeared to be always afternoon, or at the earliest the luncheon hour. All of its frequenters seemed to have plenty of leisure. A smell of old books and stale houses pervaded the Row. There was not much ventilation or light, as the upper stories of some of the shops overhung the way beneath and approached closely to one another across the street.

Most of the shops were devoted to the sale of books both old and new, and others to the sale of things you could not buy elsewhere in London. The old books were displayed in wooden trough-like boxes outside the shops. It was always exciting to hunt through these, though as a rule they only contained technical works, books of sermons and statistics, and such dry provender. There was always a chance of finding something of value, dropped in by accident, perhaps.

Tom officiously advised examining these very completely but I wanted a brand-new book, with illustrations if possible, for my birthday present. As usual, Tom won the argument, and I had for my present an old and tattered copy of a romance called *The Castle of Ehrenstein*. Tom assured me that I should never regret the purchase and undertook to read it for me first. I did not quite see the point of this, but his good intentions were apparent. There was another advantage afforded by the transaction, one which I probably should not have had in buying a new book. There was some change left over from my shilling, which we were able to spend on some fruit in Clare Market nearby. Tom was right. I never regretted the choice we had made. It was the cause of one of the most exciting adventures of my boyhood.

Some days after, when Tom had read the book and I was about to begin the first chapter, he approached me furtively, first looking back over his shoulder to see that no one else was within hearing.

"Don't be frightened," he whispered mysteriously into my ear. "I have an awful secret to tell you. Nobody else knows about it, and I can only tell you if you promise faithfully not to reveal it to a soul."

I was deeply impressed, and promised on my oath not to say a word to anybody about it.

"I've made a terrific discovery," he told me. "This house is built on an old castle which is haunted. I've already explored the banqueting hall, old dungeons and torture chambers. The chains are still hanging on the walls, so there is no doubt what the chambers were used for."

I was thrilled.

"If you can get into the castle, couldn't you take me with you?" I asked.

"Yes," he replied. "I want to show you all these wonderful things; but there is one condition I am forced to make. You must be blindfolded."

"But what's the good of my going with you, if I can't see anything?" I complained.

"Oh, you needn't bother your head about that," he answered. "I'll explain everything as we go along. Then you won't need to see them."

I had to be content with this, and an appointment was made for the following evening in the passage by the kitchen. This, he told me, was not far from the entrance to the castle he had discovered. He said that he could not say more. When the time came for the adventure I was a little afraid, but kept the appointment punctually. Tom was already there, and fortunately no one else except Boss, the black cat, who seemed to sense the mystery in the air. A handkerchief was tied over my eyes, and various passes were solemnly made in front of me to test the effectiveness of the binding. When all was ready I was turned round so many times that I did not know in which direction I was facing.

My heart was beating loudly as we started off. After passing along a gallery (as Tom called it), we stopped.

"I now press a secret spring," my guide announced, "and in the wall a stone rolls slowly back, revealing the entrance to the castle. Through the ages this has sunk so low that we must enter upon our hands and knees."

I negotiated this quite successfully without bumping my head.

"We are now in the main corridor that leads to the banqueting hall," said Tom in a subdued voice.

Tom's Castle

The corridor proved to be very crooked, and frequently turned back on itself. I questioned Tom about this peculiarity, and he replied, after advising me to talk as quietly as possible, that the twists in the passage were contrived by the old baron who owned the castle long ago, in order to baffle any enemy who might have gained an entrance to the stronghold. I could quite see the wisdom of this. Though not an enemy, I was certainly baffled.

Presently a door was opened.

"We are now in the banqueting hall," Tom said. "On the right you see the dais—at least you would see it if you weren't blindfolded. Down the centre of the hall is a long oaken table at which the serfs had their meals. A rusted dagger can still be seen on a table beneath the musician's gallery."

We retraced our steps along the crooked passage and came to stairs.

"These," said Tom, "lead to the turret, and to the chamber in which the princess was imprisoned and died from starvation. Her ghost still comes forth to haunt the castle."

"Must we explore the turret?" I asked nervously, but Tom assured me encouragingly: "No harm can touch you, so long as I am near."

We mounted the stairs and found ourselves at the door of the princess's chamber. I fancied I heard my mother's voice in conversation behind the door, but Tom hurried me away.

"The ghost is about to haunt the castle," he told me, "and it would be fatal if she saw us." We hurried down the stairs.

"Now," said Tom, "I will take you to the deepest dungeons."

He led me down and down until at the bottom of the last flight of stairs we entered a small chamber, which, even through the handkerchief, smelt cold and damp.

"This is the deepest dungeon of all," I was informed. "You will notice the bones crunching beneath your feet."

They felt rather like coals, but as I was blindfolded and my brother was not, he must have been right. Leaving the dungeon, we now proceeded along another winding passage. This seemed interminable, but at last we came to a sudden halt. Tom muttered an oath.

"Odds bodikins!" he said. "We can go no farther. The gallery is blocked by a huge carved-oak chest, with a human skull on top of it."

This was alarming, and I clutched his arm.

"No harm is done," he comforted me, "but this is a sign that our time is up and we must return."

We hurried along a seemingly endless series of passages, until at last we crawled through the secret doorway. Tom untied the handkerchief, and I found myself outside the kitchen door. Boss blinked knowingly up at us.

CHAPTER FOUR

School

IN the last chapter I have tried to show the important part played in my education by my life at home. I now hope to describe the part played by my life at school. To do this, it will be necessary to retrace my steps and begin this chapter at an earlier time; at a time when, as a younger family, we lived in a smaller house in a smaller street.

An epoch-marking day at this early stage of my career was when, amidst the congratulations of the family and their smiles of encouragement, I came down to breakfast in my first pair of breeches. The next in importance was certainly the day when I started my school education. This day marked the beginning of a new stage. Life was about to begin in earnest.

The school was on the opposite side of the road, and I was escorted on this first occasion, in a state of trepidation, by an old family nurse. She had been with our family at the time of my birth, and in virtue of her long service and care of me, when I was so little able to care for myself, she exercised a sort of proprietary right over my person. At my christening she strongly objected that not enough water had been used; some other quite ordinary children, christened at the same time, being treated more liberally in this respect. For this reason, perhaps, she henceforth devoted her life to making up for this rather feeble beginning to my spiritual career.

"Miss Mole's" was the name of the Dame school to which I was taken. The staff consisted of Miss Mole and her mother. These ladies divided their time between housekeeping duties, the education of a few young children of the neighbourhood, and the care of Mr. Mole, Miss Mole's brother. He was a smart young man with a dignified manner. He was only to be seen occasionally. We sometimes used to arrive in the morning as he was about to leave for the city, Miss Mole seeing him off, brushing his coat and putting on a few finishing touches. He was too manly to take notice of us, and we, regarding him with awe, wondered what he did in the city. No doubt something very important; for he was always arrayed in top-hat and frock-coat, and wore light kid gloves.

One of my earliest memories is of Mrs. Mole, a bent old lady in a white cap and dark apron. Her old knotted fingers and crinkled nails pointed out the letters in Mavor's Spelling Book. She would read to us the stories of Jane Bond, who had a kind face, and of many another juvenile heroine or hero. The system at Miss Mole's was in no way irksome and we had enough time left over from our tasks to amuse ourselves by drawing on our slates.

In course of time, when the family increased, we moved into a larger house in a larger street nearby. In this street dwelt my grandfather, the patriarch of the Robinsons. His home at this time was still the headquarters of the family, until eventually the members that composed the household were all dispersed. But for many years yet the unity of the clan was maintained by means of a great party held in our grandfather's home at Christmas, when all members of the family, with their wives, husbands and children would be present. Besides the Robinsons, there were many other large families in our street. We all knew one another and, as is usual with large families, had much in common. On summer evenings the street would be full of playing children.

Two old Italians with a piano organ used to appear regularly once a week and enliven us with some rattling music. We looked for them every Saturday evening. They were very dirty and very friendly and seemed as glad to see us as we were to see them. I am sure they gave us an extra share of their time and music in return for the small pittance they received from us. At the end of their performance, they would bow, raise their hats and, with other friendly gestures, pass on.

I was now old enough to go to a more advanced school, whither Tom and Charles had preceded me. The school was distant about a mile from our home. Our way lay through a poor district. The road we took was a continuation of our road but separated from it by a row of white posts, close to Cripps the grocer's where we bought our chocolate creams. Beyond this barrier, evidences of poverty began to appear and increased until we reached the corner of a slum-like street which was a veritable Alsatia. By this we always hurried. Beyond again were the cavernous railway arches, beneath which many a savage fight, fought to the knock-out blow, took place between the ragged champions of the district. We made this journey four times a day, except on rainy days, when we took our lunch to school. It was no easier in those days than now to foretell the weather. I remember that one morning, without any warning, the rain began to fall when we were at school. By midday, when the school was dispersed, it was pouring down. We were hungry and cold, and to make matters worse the rain dripped from the roof of the cloakroom in which we waited for the weather to change. Presently there was a great commotion on the stairs, and our guardian angel, in the form of our stout old servant, appeared. Red-faced and breathing heavily with the haste she had made, she burst upon us, carrying in her apron three parcels wrapped in table napkins.

Overcome by the apparition, we were at first a little shy at this intrusion of our domestic life into our public life at school. But finding that our companions were not by any means inclined to scoff and were as interested as ourselves, we examined our parcels. Each contained a meat pie, still smoking hot, and a fruit tart. We lost no time in tackling them, and our friends were not backward in helping us in this luscious work. There was plenty for us all.

The school building was composed of three dwelling-houses joined together. There was no playground, and we played in the streets outside the school. Consequently, most of our games were what may be called street games. Of these a favourite was "Tip-cat". It was played with a piece of firewood, taken from the kitchen, with each end sharpened thus: One of the pointed ends would be struck sharply with a stick, causing the cat to leap, and the player showed his skill by hitting it again in mid air and sending it as far as possible.

Another popular game was "Wogle". Why it was called "Wogle" I could never learn. I do not clearly remember the rules of the game, but it was a kind of double Tip-cat, and was played in much the same way as cricket. The wickets were two circles marked on the road about twelve feet apart, and the tip-cat was used instead of a ball. The wickets were defended with sticks.

Tip-cat

"Jolly Little Knacker" was also an exciting game. It was a leaping game, but instead of leaping over, the object was to leap on to a boy's back and stay there while a rhyme was recited: "Jolly Little Knacker, One, Two, Three!" This was made more difficult by two or three boys mounting the same horse, which sometimes broke down under the weight. There would then be a heap of struggling boys on the pavement. This was very enjoyable. Besides the usual games, such as leap-frog and the many games that can be played with marbles and peg-tops, we had "Red Rover", "Hunt the Stag", "Robbers and Thieves", "Chevy Chase", "Egg Cap", "Cherry Ogg" and "Buttons". The latter game required skill and was played by pitching brace buttons from the kerb to one of the lines marking the joints of the paving stones. The player whose button was nearest to the line took the losers' buttons.

One young gambler, having lost his all, cut the brace buttons from the trousers he was wearing. His ill-luck still pursuing him, he lost even these and returned home a sadder lad, with his hands in his empty pockets, and his braces dangling uselessly.

In the late summer and autumn, Cherry Ogg, played with cherry stones, and Conkers were the favourites. I do not remember exactly how Cherry Ogg was played, but it was a game of greed, and the pockets of the successful player would bulge with his stony wealth. A capitalist and a miser in his

Egg Cap

way, he gained no glory by his victories. Often he had a cloth bag to carry his gains.

There was something more romantic about Conkers. The name, I believe, means " Conquerors ". Like the knights-errant of old, the victorious conker always added to his own achievements those of his conquered opponents. I can remember an old horse chestnut, battered and scarred, on the end of a piece of frayed string. Its owner was envied by everyone in the school. There was nearly a rebellion when the doughty old nut was taken from its owner, who happened to be displaying it during school hours. It was ignominiously thrown amongst a miscellaneous clutter of confiscated goods; half-eaten apples,

Conkers

a piece of toffee, marbles and peg-tops. " Sic transit gloria . . . ."

In the winter, for the sake of warmth, we had more active games, and bowling hoops was much favoured. I think they held their popularity until the bicycle took their place many years after. Our hoop clubs were well organized institutions, and in full parade they were impressive, if rather noisy. These games were all strictly seasonal. No boy would dream of bowling a hoop in June or pitting his conker against all-comers in the spring. You might as well hope to play snowballs in August. In the winter Cherry Ogg was off, and remained nothing more than a sad memory until the following fruit season. But in many cases it would be difficult to explain why a certain game was played only at a particular season, or what authority ruled these matters.

The education I received at this school, although on the whole of a meagre character, had some advantages. I certainly managed to learn to read and write, which, after all, are accomplishments worth having. I also learnt some very elementary arithmetic, a little history and geography. My head was never worried with foreign or dead languages, which perhaps

The Hoop Club

was good for it at that time of mental confusion. The teachers, with one exception did not inspire me with a wish to learn; no doubt I appeared very dull, and it is possible that I did not inspire them with any wish to teach.

The exception was a mistress, who, I believe, had a genius for teaching. She certainly had the advantage of teaching me a subject which I had never approached before, and of beginning at its most elementary stage. But so truly did she lay the foundations that little difficulty was felt in the further development of the subject. Every step forward was made from a well-secured position, and the new position was consolidated. Beyond this, she had the art of inspiring interest in the subject she taught, and a friendly personality that made it a pleasure to satisfy her. The subject, strangely enough, was electricity and magnetism. The interest aroused by this teacher's methods gave me the first real satisfaction I derived from my school education.

I sometimes flatter myself with the thought that having made so promising a beginning I might in the end have become a great scientist. Unfortunately, or fortunately for the world of science, I left the school before these studies had advanced beyond the rudimentary stage, and they were never resumed.

There were little or no classical studies, but many branches of science were taught; physiology, chemistry, electricity and magnetism. We had an impressive array of apparatus, such as retorts, Leyden jars, batteries, magnets and electrical machines of various kinds. Interesting and odoriferous experiments were carried out. The headmaster was greatly interested in all these subjects, and I can remember a lecture of his in which he prophesied that some day telegrams would be sent without wires. That was at least fifty-five years ago.

One of our masters was a very old gentleman, who delighted in propounding to the boys his own theory of the evolution of man. " It is all nonsense," he said, " to imagine that man was descended from the apes. Of course not; he was descended from the bear." I do not think we were very interested in any case, but he proceeded to prove his theory by comparative anatomy. We did not understand his arguments, but were quite prepared to take his word for it. He was a kind, but obstinate and fussy old man. Quite innocent of any intention to commit an injustice, he would often, through shortsightedness, punish the wrong boy, and no one could persuade him of his error. However, he was very popular. I can remember that when at last he announced his retirement into private life, we all subscribed and presented him with a gold watch. It bore a suitable inscription, expressing our appreciation of his long and unwearying services. The ceremony was an affecting one and took place before the assembled school. After a short and complimentary speech by the headmaster, each one of us shook hands with our departing friend. We were naturally somewhat taken aback at the beginning of the next term to find him back in his place again, as fussy and busy as ever. When at last he did leave, nobody suggested that he should be given another gold watch.

The schoolmaster

It was so often my misfortune to miss the beginning and foundation of the subjects I was taught at school, or not to have them deeply impressed upon me before passing on. Whether this was only my own particular misfortune I have no means of telling, but in my case it resulted in mental confusion and lack of interest. Like most children of my age, I was eager and curious, and waiting to be interested; but I must confess that my schools rarely supplied this want. On fitting occasions I received physical punishment, and very likely deserved it, though I never admitted it at the time. But I was never cruelly punished. The harm that may result from a want of system in teaching is of a more subtle kind. In this way many hours of the most sensitive and impressionable time of a child's life may be squandered and worried away. Education at that time, however, was not regarded scientifically, and my conscientious, if misguided, teachers had more excuse for their failures than the teachers of to-day.

The rebuke

" All in " was the general cry when the wooden door at the side of the house was opened at half-past nine. We all left our games, cramming into our pockets the peg-tops, marbles, tip-cats or whatever we were playing with, and climbed the stairs into school. Our caps and coats were hung in what used to be a greenhouse. The flowers had long since departed. The school was a mixed school, and when the boys were all assembled in their various classrooms, the girls would troop in and take their seats and the lessons would begin. During the morning the headmaster's wife would proceed solemnly through the school to collect any fees that might have been brought by the pupils. I remember one boy whose parents had delayed payment unreasonably. He was sent home to fetch the money. He did not seem to mind in the least, and presently returned with the fee and smilingly resumed his lessons.

Peg-tops

The headmaster was a portly gentleman, and besides possessing a dignified bearing, he had many letters after his name. What they meant we did not know, but they were very impressive. His majestic presence earned the respect of all his pupils, and in one at least inspired awe to an almost overpowering extent. He had a large family, and one of his sons was a great friend of mine. I can remember being invited to tea one afternoon, and being so overcome at seeing the great man drinking tea in the bosom of his family like any ordinary person that I could not keep my gaze from him. Even here he did not unbend, but maintained his dignity as a headmaster by reading a learned work while we were chattering. My gaze, however, was so fixed that whenever his eyes wandered from his book to his tea, as they frequently did, they invariably caught mine. Before the end of the meal this scrutiny became so embarrassing to him that at last his dignity failed him. Closing his book sharply, he met my gaze squarely and made a most unheadmasterlike grimace. He then got up from his chair and left the room.

He was proud of his school, and I think we were proud of belonging to it, especially when we marched through the streets to the local hall where our annual school concerts and prize-givings were held. We were almost military as we proceeded in double file. Pride in our school was aroused as we looked backwards at the long line we formed. Our establishment was called a college, and we considered ourselves superior to the ordinary schools of the neighbourhood. These pretensions excited envy, and war would sometimes break out. Other schools would unite against us, and there were great rushings backwards and forwards through the streets, but seldom any actual meetings. Sometimes a kind of guerrilla warfare would be waged for days; but it was rarely that anything worse happened than a misdirected barrage of stones which, thrown from a safe distance, did little damage—at any rate to the combatants.

In virtue of our greater respectability, our headmaster insisted on some insignia to distinguish us. School ties were not worn in those days, and it was thought fitting that we, as pupils of a college, should wear what we called college caps—what are generally called mortar-boards. They are good hats in any case, and serviceable even when the board, through frequent battery, has come off. They added dignity to the procession when we paraded through the streets to attend some function in state.

The great occasion of the year was the School Concert and Prize-giving.

Mivvies an

School

The whole school would then turn out in its full strength, to show what it was worth and the great things it could do when put to it. The hall was filled with the fathers, mothers, aunts and friends of the young collegians; the parents waving their programmes and in other ways trying eagerly to attract the attention of their children on the crowded platform. They were proud to see them in this exalted position, and taking part in the great festival; for it was nothing less.

At one side of the platform was the piano, at the other a table piled high with the prizes. They were mostly books. It was tantalizing to look at their bright new covers and to wonder if one of them was for myself. The list of the prize-winners was kept an inviolable secret until the presentation. Behind the table was a row of chairs, now occupied by respectable and distinguished ladies and gentlemen of the district. Very pleasant were they all, shaking hands with one another and smiling benignantly at the children. Behind these good people the children sat on tiers of seats raised one above the other. The whole of the cheerful view was closed in on each side by palms and flowers.

The headmaster stepped forward, tapped sharply with his baton on the stand in front of the platform. Silence followed. The programme was about to begin. It was opened by the Cantata conducted by the headmaster himself. For weeks before we had been practising it, first in Tonic Sol Fa form, the headmaster being an enthusiastic advocate of that system, and then with the words to the tunes we had learned. With what zest we now sang " Merrily, merrily, dance and sing; Drive all fears, all cares away!" We could have danced merrily enough, and we certainly had followed the latter part of this good advice for the time being.

The Cantata was followed by one or two plays of an amusing character, and some speeches, but the grand climax of the evening's entertainment was the distribution of prizes by the Member of Parliament or his wife or the vicar or someone else of local importance. There were so many prizes and

Glassies

certificates that the majority of the pupils received something. It must not be thought, on this account, that every one of them was not deserved. There was no doubt of this from the loudness of the applause that greeted each recipient, and the joyful way in which he or she was congratulated by the Member of Parliament or whoever it was that distributed the prizes.

To finish the evening, bouquets were given, more complimentary speeches were made, votes of thanks proposed and last of all we sang " God save the Queen ". It was very warm at the end of the entertainment, but this did not matter. It was so delightful and everyone was pleased with everyone else.

Dignity and Impudence

Tired out, I would go home with my parents, perhaps the proud possessor of a prize.

When I was about twelve years old, I was sent to the Islington High School, whither my brothers Tom and Charles had preceded me. This school was founded in 1830, and was then known as the Proprietary School of Islington. To quote the rules, the object of the school was " to provide a course of Education for Youth, to comprise Classical Learning, the Modern Languages, Mathematics and such other branches of Useful Knowledge as may be advantageously introduced; together with religious and moral instruction, in conformity with the doctrines and discipline of the Church of England." It was more expensive than the school which I had left and had some pretensions to being a public school. Most of the masters had university degrees, and wore caps and gowns when teaching. This impressed me very much at first.

The object in sending us to this school was to add a final polish to our education and give it a more classical tone than could be acquired at our former school. I cannot say that in my case this end was attained. Tom and Charles did well enough, and when I arrived had already distinguished themselves. Whether I started in the middle of a term and could not make up for the time thus lost, I cannot remember. My fate still pursuing me, I rarely seemed to start at the beginning of my subjects or, if I did, to be well grounded in them. Much of the time I spent at this school was in this manner thrown away.

Perhaps, after all this time, I am inclined in my mind to exaggerate my failure. I find in a report of this period that I was not merely good, but V. Good, in Geography and History; Fair in Reading, and that I showed Good Ability and Progress in Free-Hand Drawing. I am glad to think that I was at one time of my life V. Good in Geography. Quite a different formula would be necessary to describe my present proficiency in this interesting subject.

We had now moved into a larger house in Camden Road. This was too far from the school to allow us to come home in the middle of the day, and we had to depend, for our midday meal, on a few sandwiches or what a few pence could buy. It is true we had a large dinner awaiting us in the evening on our return from school, but I used to envy those boys who had more pence than I and who could afford a larger scone with butter and a cup of coffee. I envied even more those fortunate boys who had the hot dinner provided by the school. This envy would not have been so great if a tantalizing smell of cooking had not been allowed to steal into the playground in the middle of the day.

This problem of feeding, not through any want of trying by my parents, was never satisfactorily solved until the intervention of a good friend. The failure may have been partly the cause of much of my discontent, and the disappointing results of my efforts, and, at times, my lack of effort.

Though few happy memories remain to me of this school, I have to thank it for the beginning of my friendship with Fred Bernard Smith; a friendship which after so many years is still as strong as it was in those far-off days. I cannot recall how our friendship began, but I do not forget that his good mother, realizing my plight and the difficulties of my parents, befriended me. She had a house of business which she superintended near the school, and at which there was a generous spread every day for the staff. Fred had his dinner here and now I was invited to share it. A good thick cut of roast mutton, vegetables and plenty of gravy, followed by a roly-poly suet pudding bursting with strawberry jam, make a better foundation for your education than can be laid by the best of scones and butter.

Another of our school companions, whose friendship has remained with us till to-day, was Richard Walthew, the composer. He was more particularly a friend of my brother Tom. He was a frequent visitor to our home. His playing was a source of great pleasure and wonder to us as we gathered round him at the piano.

We all admired his single-hearted devotion to his work and his boyish intolerance of all he considered false or merely pretentious in the music of the day, but this was after we left school. I am not qualified to write of his musical achievements since, but they include a musical setting of " The Pied Piper ", which he composed early in his career. I can remember how much we loved to hear him play extracts from it. He composed many songs. I prided myself on my rendering of " Eldorado ", but whether the composer was equally thrilled is another matter. His duet setting of " It was a lover and his lass ", and particularly his music to the comic opera " The Enchanted Island ", which has been performed three times at the B.B.C., were amongst his more popular works. The libretto for the last of these was written by R. H. V. Bloor. In recent years Richard Walthew has devoted himself to chamber music. He will be known to many music lovers by his association with the South Place Sunday Popular Concerts.

I can only imagine the environment of his life from an occasional visit I made to his home in Highbury Place, but it was surely conducive to the growth of his strong predilection for music. To enter Highbury Place about fifty years ago was like stepping into the days of Jane Austen. An old history of Islington describes Highbury Place as " one of the finest rows of houses in the environs of the Metropolis: it is chiefly inhabited by merchants and other persons of opulence, connected with the trades of the City ". Although it may have fallen a little from this high estate, it still preserved something of its old exclusiveness. It was approached through a row of white posts. After the noise and traffic of Upper Street and Holloway Road there was a restful calm about the Place, and its old Georgian houses. They overlooked a green meadow, upon which a flock of sheep would sometimes be feeding. The meadow was separated from the Place by a fence of neat white posts connected with one another by black chains. The lives of the dwellers in the Place seemed to accord with their environment. My friend Percy Billinghurst lived a few doors away from the Walthews. I can remember visiting him too and listening to his old blind father playing the organ. After, we would walk in the garden and examine the mulberry tree of which Bill (my friend) was very proud. Before I left, a jug of foaming ale drawn from a wooden cask in the deep cellars of Highbury Place would be put before us. Two tumblers were placed beside it as a gentle hint, if we needed one, of the use to which it was to be put—a hint we lost no time in taking. In such surroundings lived two of the oldest friends of the Robinsons.

CHAPTER FIVE

Holidays

THE alternation of school and home life was not without variation. We had many outings and holidays. As soon as the days grew longer, and summer was in the air, we began to look forward to our seaside holiday, which we usually spent at Ramsgate. This expedition was a serious undertaking for my mother, upon whose shoulders most of the responsibility rested. Preparations would be in hand for weeks before. As the time drew near our excitement became intense. There were new clothes to be bought and fitted, new sand-shoes and new hats to be tried on. So many new things had we to wear that we felt quite new ourselves.

When the day arrived, we travelled to the railway station in a four-wheeled cab. Our luggage and the perambulator were packed on top and we were packed inside. Our progress seemed far too slow. Certainly the driver had a load on his mind as well as on his cab, and he refused to be hurried. Admittedly he was not going to the seaside, but we were exasperated by his lack of the holiday spirit. However, he brought us safely to the Holborn Viaduct Station. We travelled by the London, Chatham and Dover Railway. Our dread of missing the train was removed only when the tickets were bought and we were sitting on the hard seats of the carriage. We had some anxious moments when we saw our perambulator, apparently neglected, on a distant part of the platform. Stowing the luggage seemed a leisurely process, but in spite of their seeming casualness the porters did not fail us.

For the whole of the journey my face was at the carriage window. London seemed to be a vast city of roofs and chimney-pots. We could see into attics, in which people were doing everyday things, strangely unmindful of seaside holidays. Gradually the smoke and grime of London gave place to the green of the countryside. A sunlit panorama of downs and woods, fields and villages slid past. When at length we were becoming a little weary of these sights, there was a cry of " The sea!" and we all crowded to the side of the carriage from which it could be seen. At the same time the window was lowered, and a sweet smell of fresh sea air drifted in.

Charles Lamb, as a boy, was disappointed with the sea. He expected too much from it. Yet I can remember one boy, at least, whose expectations were great, and who was not disappointed. We were thrilled by the sight of that distant horizon, and the sun shining on a sail far away.

In good time we arrived at Ramsgate. Our luggage was stacked on the platform, and we waited by it while my father went into the town to find lodgings. It may seem to us to-day a very casual way of proceeding, leaving so important a matter as finding our lodgings until after our arrival. But we do not seem to have suffered by it. He was so long away that we began to worry and to picture ourselves spending the night in the station. Our anxiety was relieved at last, and we accompanied him to our quarters, followed by a porter with a barrow heaped with our luggage. We knew a few of the natives of Ramsgate. Old Hogbin, the ex-captain of the lifeboat, who could tell us of many a wreck on the Goodwin Sands, greeted us when we met him by the harbour. His son George, and the daughter who kept a public house, were also glad to see us. Much shopping had to be done on this first evening. There were spades, pails and bathing drawers to be bought, besides provisions for the morrow. It was not until the next morning that we got down to the serious business of enjoying our holiday.

Our breakfast consisted of a savoury dish of fried dabs and plaice cooked in toasted breadcrumbs. Our appetites were sharpened, for we had been out in the keen air of the early morning with my father, to buy the fish in the market. It had only at that moment arrived from the boats. After breakfast we trooped down to the sands to start our campaign of pleasure, with our spades, pails, bathing drawers and towels. The sands were crowded, and the children were amusing themselves in much the same way as they do to-day at the seaside. There were no huts or bathing tents, and the few who bathed did so decorously from a bathing machine run well out into the water. The scene was not enlivened by many-coloured bathing costumes, but it was gay enough in the bright sunlight. The women and children all wore clothes of cheerful colours, and the men were clad in white flannels or light check suits.

The entertainments on the sands were of a simple character. We had no fun-fairs, great wheels, or other Blackpool thrills. We had no concert parties, but we were sufficiently amused by a troop of minstrels and by Punch and Judy. The silhouette-cutter always did a good business. Without considering him a charlatan, we were a little supercilious towards his artistic pretensions. I can remember my father borrowing his scissors and offering to cut his portrait. I do not think the professional quite liked this inversion of his usual procedure. He doubtless felt as Rembrandt would have felt if the Captain of the Night Watch had offered to paint his portrait. However, he could not refuse what amounted to a challenge. To do so would have implied a fear of comparison. He got out of his difficulty very well by condescendingly admiring my father's work as that of a promising amateur.

The photographer, too, was always busy with his little portable darkroom, into which he tucked his head when developing. We wondered what mysterious operations went on in this magic box. I once tried to peep into the tiny yellow window, but was soon made to understand that this sort of thing was not allowed. He had no need to advertise, as a musty smell of concentrated "hypo" or some other photographic chemical proclaimed his presence for yards around. In those days there were no instantaneous photographs, at least on Ramsgate sands. It was difficult to stand still in front of the rickety tripod for so long, but it was wonderful to have your portrait taken on tin and framed in gold while you waited.

Condescendingly admiring my father's work

Although at the time these holidays seemed to be full of excitement, in retrospect they seem to have followed a tranquil course. However, one or two incidents have stuck in my memory.

No one, with the exception of Jonah, has been swallowed by a whale and lived to talk about it. My brother Charles was nearly swallowed by a whale, and talked very much about it afterwards. He was justly proud of this distinction, and we, while affecting to make light of the matter, secretly envied him. But we shared a kind of reflected glory. An old whale, apparently dead, was washed up on the sands. There was great excitement, and people crowded to see it. One of the boatmen, in playful mood, lifted Charles from the ground and seated him on the monster's head. To everyone's surprise it was found to be alive, but this last indignity was too much for it. The whale gave a monstrous gasp, and a final heave shook its whole body as it expired. Charles was sent sprawling on the sands. As he stoutly maintained, no one could doubt the intention of the whale to end its ill-spent life by making a meal of him.

The photograph

My father, true to his love of the sea and of ships, which love he longed to communicate to us, enjoyed rowing us round the inside of the harbour. Hidden from the frivolity of the holiday-makers on the sands, here the real business of the sea was carried on. It was a fine old harbour with a lighthouse at the entrance, through which we could see the open sea. This was not the sea beside which we bathed and paddled with our toy boats, but the sea across which sailed the great ships from foreign lands to the shelter here to be found. Here one would be loading or unloading its cargo at the quay, there another would be taking on stores for a continuation of its voyage. Some of the vessels would have French crews, and my father, who could speak a little of their language, would exchange jokes with them as we rowed round their craft. One day the battered remains of a ship that had been wrecked on the Goodwin Sands in a recent storm was towed into the harbour. Its tangled rigging, cluttered decks and shorn masts brought home to us the cruel anger that sometimes possessed this peaceful sea.

Adventure had an attraction for us and led us on one occasion to attempt a more daring voyage than usual. We proposed to row round the outside wall of the harbour into its entrance. This wanted some seamanship, and we engaged a cheerful old boatman to act as pilot and captain. The whole family embarked from the sands, and at first all went very merrily. The boatman proved to be the merriest of us all. So merry did he become that we had to admit that he was not as sober as one should be in his responsible position. To negotiate the outermost point of the harbour, we found it necessary to hoist a sail. Our pilot carried out this manœuvre so recklessly that he nearly landed, or rather dipped, us in difficulties. I have a vivid memory of our too-cheerful boatman struggling to recapture the flapping canvas, while the boat whirled round in the current. With the help of a kindly providence he brought us eventually into the calm waters of the harbour. We joked about it afterwards, but my father resolved to trust in future to his own navigation.

In the quiet of the evening, we would take a leisurely walk over the cliffs towards Pegwell Bay or Broadstairs. Then, tired out with the sweet tiredness that only sea air and holiday activities can bring, we would return through fields of corn. After supper, when the children and all anxieties concerning them were put to rest, my father and mother used to stroll down to the harbour. The road leading from there was lined with flare-lit stalls, where, on clean white cloths, oysters, whelks and other succulent shell-fish were temptingly displayed. All ready to be eaten, they were set out on little plates, flanked by bottles of vinegar, pepper pots, and stacks of new white bread and fresh butter. On special occasions one of us was allowed to go with them on these appetizing walks, and to taste with them these cool delicacies.

Sometimes we were sent to stay with distant relatives at Brighton, perhaps to be out of the way at the birth of a brother or sister, or to recover from some childish illness. These relatives lived in a little street leading off from the front at the east end of the town. It was a narrow street through which the wind swept fiercely to the downs at the back. You could smell the sea in every room of the house. Every house in the street had an announcement of appartments to let displayed in one of its windows.

As these visits rarely coincided with the Brighton season we saw an aspect of the town unfamiliar to holiday visitors. The inhabitants were not devoting their lives entirely to the pleasure of other people, but for the time being lived for themselves. There were a few visitors even now, such as stay through most of the year. These consisted of invalids, of retired army officers and their wives, or members of some colonial service, seeking to regain the health they had lost abroad. There were some lonely boys and girls, too, whose parents lived in climates too unhealthy for their children.

Our friend Charlie Greenfield

I can remember one bleak fortnight in March. It must have been when George was born. It was cold and windy, and the sea was always rough. There was no paddling or bathing to amuse us, but long rambles on the stony beach, and over the cliffs towards Rottingdean. Our objective on these walks was an old tumbledown hut, originally put up for the shelter of shepherds. We would rest here awhile, and after assisting the work of the storms and winds by pulling down a few more planks, we would return. One of our companions on these expeditions was a shaggy-haired young tramp whom we knew by the name of Charlie Greenfield. He was a cheerful soul, and we believed that he smoked dried seaweed and slept out of doors under the lee of one of the great black fishing-smacks on the beach.

This bleak season did not detract from the fascination that the old Chain

Pier had for us. We visited it whenever our pocket money allowed us to do so. Walking between the little kiosks at the bases of the great stanchions that supported the chains was like walking the deck of a ship. In windy weather it swayed slightly like a ship at sea. Even at this time of year you could buy brandy-balls and bull's-eyes at some of the kiosks; at others, polished pebbles, and pin-cushions and work-boxes decorated with coloured sea-shells were displayed, together with views of Brighton. The end of the pier, also, had a nautical air, and we pretended that we were voyaging on some stout old wooden ship. The illusion was helped by the many masts and flag-staffs, and by the noise made by their ropes as they flapped against them in the wind. This part of the pier was mostly constructed of great weather-worn timbers. Even the bandstand might have been the work of a ship-wright.

Underneath the end of the pier, and supporting the upper deck, was a forest of wooden piles and iron ties, encrusted with shells and hung with seaweed. A platform of iron gratings ran round the end of the pier. To enter this weird underworld, you descended the mere skeleton of a stairway. Standing on the platform you gazed through the grating at your feet and all around you at the sea. Another iron stairway led from here without any compromise straight down into the depths of the water. I never believed the story of the silk-hatted gentleman who was said to have come up these stairs from out of the sea and walked calmly away. A dim green light penetrated this eerie world amongst the bones of the old pier. In stormy weather there was pandemonium down here, as the waves swelled up the sides of the great piles, and then, with an angry hiss, subsided, leaving their flanks streaming with water.

Neither the shabby splendour of the Royal Pavilion, the Aquarium, nor the Museum, with its bottles of Dead Sea water, had such an attraction for us as this old pier, which at last succumbed to the storms. The Brighton of my childhood resembled far more closely the bleak watering-place of Dombey and Son than the gay Brighton of to-day.

Besides these seaside holidays, we had shorter outings. Of these, one of the most enjoyable was the Sunday School treat. We attended the Sunday School with just sufficient regularity to qualify for the treat. On the appointed day, eight or nine wagonettes assembled outside the school. Each of them was gaily decked with flags and streamers and had a brightly striped awning for protection against sun and rain. The children arrived in the early morning for we had a long way to go. We were dressed in our gayest clothes, and each carried a parcel of sandwiches and cakes. Two long benches, facing one another, ran the length of each wagonette, and on to these the children crowded. It was a close fit, and we had to turn half round in our seats to see outside.

There were many parents and friends to send us on our way rejoicing. The horses tossed their heads, impatient to start. It was a spirited scene when the long cavalcade at last moved off in the brilliant early-morning sunshine. The children leant out, waving their hands, shouting and singing; the driver and the man on the step at the back of each wagonette entered into the spirit of the thing, and seemed prepared to make a day of it. We were followed by a crowd of poor ragged boys, who, debarred from the wagonettes, intended to accompany us on foot. After a joyful and very hot morning, riding along the dusty country roads, we arrived at our destination in Epping Forest. We left the wagonettes and, crossing a style, entered an emerald meadow. It was sprinkled with vast constellations of buttercups and daisies, and walled in on almost every side by the forest.

Many games were arranged for the afternoon—rounders, running races and jumping. Prizes were not forgotten for the winners. But these were not for me. The forest had a lure I could not resist. When the teachers who had us in their care were busily superintending the games, I cautiously climbed the fence at the edge of the field and entered the forest. I at once became an intrepid explorer. My only weapon was a short stick, but I was ready to meet any foe, man or beast. My courage was high as I crouched beneath a bush, prepared to spring upon a lion or a wild Indian, should any be lurking in undergrowth.

It was delightfully cool beneath the tall forest trees, and I was tempted to wander farther into the wood. I boldly pushed on through open glades and dense coppices, where I had to bend low beneath the overhanging branches. The afternoon wore on, and the sun was not now so high in the sky. There was a feeling abroad in the woods of late afternoon, warning me that it was time to find my way back. I now tried to retrace my steps, but found this to be more and more difficult; instead, I seemed to go deeper and deeper into the forest.

My courage gradually oozed away, and I realized I was lost. The prospect of a night in the woods was before me, and I was beset with strange

The Boy in the Wood

fears in the silence and solitude of the trees. Presently I heard a slight sound in the woods behind me. I turned fearfully, not daring to imagine what I should see. At first, nothing came into my view, and my solitude seemed unbroken. Soon I noticed, above a bush a little distance away, a shock of red hair, crowning a little freckled face. A pair of round eyes gazed wonderingly at me. I was relieved to find that this apparition was nothing more terrifying than a country boy. He was unable to direct me, but he led me to his home, a cottage not far away. His kindly mother, hearing of my plight, gave me a glass of milk, and under her motherly guidance the intrepid explorer was taken back to his companions.

Not all Sunday School treats brought such adventures, but it is this one that I remember. Mention of Sunday School treats always brings back to me that afternoon in the woods. When tea had been eaten and all prizes won, it was time to return. Each with a large bunch of wild flowers, we took our seats in the wagonettes. The return was slower than the outward journey. The horses were tired and we were tired, but we sang sleepily all the way home. The poor ragged boys were naturally more tired than any of us. Out of pity the drivers stopped the horses and the boys were taken in, and they curled up at our feet. Some of them were fast asleep before we arrived home. We were not in much better case, when, all drowsy and sunburnt, we were met by our parents at the end of the journey.

On Saturdays we would sometimes be taken to town by our father. This was a great treat which took place usually in the summer time. In our best clothes, we walked to the corner of Holloway Road where we mounted the bus. This public conveyance was one of those since named knife-board buses. The outside passengers sat in two rows back to back along the length of the roof. In front and at either side of the driver were a few seats, usually occupied by the regular travellers who made the journey every day. It was a position of importance and one that was always taken by my father. He was considered especially entitled to it, as he knew Charlie East, the driver of the bus by which he usually travelled, quite well. The conductor stood on a little perch by the door at the back which opened and shut like a street door. There were no tickets. Although the fares were regularized, how the takings were checked was a mystery. The company must have had a sublime confidence in their servants. I believe that when tickets were introduced this measure was considered as an unkind aspersion cast upon the conductors.

We had to be helped up to our position beside my father. We climbed to this by the front wheel and a little step. It was a long journey to town. First we were taken among the familiar sights of Holloway Road, and then by Highbury Station and the Angel and through many little turnings in

Clerkenwell until eventually we arrived at our journey's end and Danes Inn. The roads were filled with horse traffic, heavy drays rumbled along and then came four-wheeled cabs, jaunty hansoms with jingling bells and dashing drivers who looked as though they knew a thing or two about horse racing. These would be followed by milk carts, a doctor's carriage, and greengrocers' carts loaded with baskets of sweet-smelling fruit. A smart equipage would dash by carrying a silk-hatted gentleman to the city. There was a strong smell of horses in the air, and we soon became used to the continuous rattle of hoofs on the granite metalled road. There were many other buses too, the outsides of which were crowded with silk-hatted gentlemen reading their morning papers. Nearly every man wore a silk hat. The passengers in front were talking to the drivers but there was only one Charlie East.

It was a great experience to ride beside Charlie. We enjoyed his repartee. We were always on his side in the witty contests with other drivers that took place along the road. How we laughed at his wordy triumphs which were ours quite as much as his.

On arriving at Danes Inn, we climbed the stone stairs that led to my father's rooms. At midday we went out to buy some ham sandwiches. We walked along the Strand. There were no law courts there in those days, and after going under Temple Bar we took our way along Fleet Street. The street was crowded, little boys were running in and out among the horses, cleaning the roads with brush and pan. It was midday dinner-time and silk-hatted and bewhiskered gentlemen were hurrying to the many eating houses along the street. From these there issued delightful smells of roast joints and vegetables. We arrived at the ham and beef shop and ordered our sandwiches. My mouth waters even now at the thought of such sandwiches. If you had no appetite at all, you would have become hungry at once to see those thick red-and-white slices carved from the fresh juicy ham. They were then placed gently between two pieces of new white bread. With these we returned to Danes Inn where we made a good meal. Our joys were not ended with this; we still had our ride home where we arrived in time for tea.

Unlike the children of to-day who go to the cinema once or twice a week, we had only one theatrical entertainment in the year. In the winter we usually went to a pantomime. To this we eagerly looked forward for weeks in advance. Being pantomime producers ourselves we understood something about it. Sometimes we would go to the Eagle in the City Road where the great George Conquest performed or to the Standard Theatre at Hoxton. At other times we would be taken to Hengler's Circus or the Mohawk Minstrels. But it was always the theatre we preferred. The most thrilling of all to us was the Standard, for it necessitated staying for a night with a distant relative who kept a public house in Whitechapel. We were half asleep after our visit to the theatre, but the public house was not closed on our return. We had to walk through the private bar. After the darkness of the four-wheeled cab which had brought us home, it was like coming suddenly from a cave into the glare of sunlight. It was a dazzling picture. The gilt mirrors, the polished mahogany counters, the stout pink-and-white bar ladies with high masses of curls and brightly coloured bodices, the tinkling glasses, and the shining faces of the many laughing customers all combined with the warm alcoholic atmosphere to form a wild dream to the dazed and sleepy children who walked through to bed.

CHAPTER SIX

Friends and a Funeral

I THINK I may reasonably claim to have been bred in an environment truly peaceful. Among my near and distant relations and friends may be numbered artists, wood engravers, and followers of many other peaceful professions.

My father's work brought him into constant contact with journalists, and as I have already mentioned, particularly with Mr. John Latey, junior, the editor of *The Penny Illustrated Paper*. Later he was to be the editor of *The Sketch* and *The Illustrated London News*. His father, Mr. John Lash Latey, had previously been the editor of the last-named journal for thirty-eight years.

Amiable fellows

Mr. John Latey, junior, will be remembered not only for his work as a journalist but as a genial and friendly personality with a large acquaintance amongst the literati of his time. George R. Sims, Augustus Sala, and Captain Mayne Reid were great friends of his. Earlier still he knew Charles Dickens and his family and many other writers of that period. He will also be known as one of the founders of the London Press Club. His son my good friend, William Lash Latey, true to the family tradition has distinguished himself as a journalist and also as a barrister. He has written some important works on law. At the time of which I am now writing we frequently met the young Latey family, with whom we were nearly contemporary, at children's parties. Our friendship was drawn closer in later years when I married the only daughter.

Amongst our friends may also be numbered many of a different category. They included sea captains, bookbinders, goldsmiths and innkeepers. There was a hatter, of whom I shall have more to say, a friendly umbrella-maker and a greengrocer, not to mention members of that thriftless tribe, amiable fellows, who follow no profession in particular and dabble in many to no purpose. Also I remember hearing of a distant relative who was a wine and spirit taster. He pursued his peaceful vocation with such zest, and cultivated such a perfect technique, that he succumbed to his exertions for the good of the wine-and-spirit trade in middle age.

Of the many artist friends whom I call to mind, there was J. Mahoney who made some good Dickens illustrations. He painted well too in a Meisonnier manner. He was an irascible Irishman with whom my father had frequent and at times violent quarrels. But the friendship was always tranquilly resumed. Also there was poor Wagner. Who knows of Wagner to-day, of his beautiful and imaginative landscapes or of his tragic poverty?

Perhaps not quite so peaceful was the hatter, who was rather a mad one, I am afraid. He was a worthy sprout on a branch of the family which emigrated to the United States many years before the time of which I am writing. Family ties were always strong with the Robinsons, and on a visit to this country he was greeted as a well-loved member of the family, although not personally known to any of us. I have always supposed that the object of his visit was to keep in touch with the ever-changing fashions of top-hats in civilized countries.

He got well away with it

Of course we entertained him, welcoming the opportunity of displaying the Robinson hospitality. Among other especially British experiences to which he was treated was Derby Day. That ever-lively occasion was still more enlivened, during a slight altercation in which he became embroiled, by his pulling out a gun which he always carried about with him. Whatever the cause of the dispute and his vigorous, wild-west gesture, he got well away with it and scattered his opponents.

We were not a little puffed up by this incident, as showing the stuff we Robinsons were really made of if you only knew, and the sort of thing we could do when properly roused.

Despite such rare outbursts of the fighting spirit I think we were more devoted to the arts of peace than of war. I can find no evidence of a professional soldier in the family archives, unless I except an old and faded photograph of a young officer in epaulettes seated uncomfortably on an ornamental chair. I have not the remotest idea who he was. He may have been only a chance acquaintance, or a mere outsider married into the family. If the latter, no doubt he was soon converted and retired from the army, overcome by the persuasions and example of his new relations. Let us hope that he ended a well-spent life as a respected and peaceful citizen with a large family of his own.

It must not be thought that I write of these matters with any pacifist bias. To my brothers and myself, at least, it must be admitted that it would have been a source of pride to have had a real soldier for an uncle or a cousin, however far removed. Whether the want of this exciting influence has coloured my after life and work, or whether it has taken all colour out of them, I must leave the reader to decide for himself.

Our young lives impinged upon the military at one point only, and there not very alarmingly. We always looked up to my uncle George Heath, who lived with us, as an elder brother and do so to-day. As a young man he was an enthusiastic volunteer. To see him every Saturday afternoon in the full military glory of his uniform was one of the excitements of the week. But to see him being equipped for the annual Easter review and sham fight on Brighton Downs was the real thing. This tremendous process was not accomplished without the willing help of most members of the household. His dark-green uniform; his spiked helmet (for butting at the enemy, we supposed); his greatcoat strapped suffocatingly to his shoulders; the general impression of strain and efficiency as, with grave danger to his blood-vessels, the various straps, bands and belts were drawn tighter and tighter with apoplectic thoroughness; all this was super-military.

It was all so strenuous

Then there was the little barrel-shaped vessel, filled with cold tea, hanging at his side, the sharp three-edged bayonet and the cold thrill at the thought of it passing through you. It was all so strenuous, grown-up and manly that as soon as the proud and rather self-conscious warrior had departed, we ourselves had to do as nearly as possible the same thing. For this purpose an old shako, the only relic of my father's volunteering days, was invaluable.

Our rare contacts with the military in the past had not always been as harmless as this. Many years before a grandfather of mine kept a country inn, much patronized by officers from a neighbouring barracks. He had a happy gift for making fortunes—a feat he accomplished three times, I am told; but it was seriously neutralized by an unhappy habit of losing them soon afterwards. He was something of a Greek and Latin scholar, and perhaps his preoccupation with Greek and Latin books was detrimental to the proper care of his cash books. At any rate, the officers were allowed to run up large bills. Their duty suddenly called them away to the Crimea, from which many of the poor fellows never returned. The bills remained unpaid, and my grandfather was forced to close the inn. Of that and the other lost fortunes all that remained was the thought that we might have been very rich, a thought from which I still try to draw some consolation.

No one could deny that we were a sociable as well as a peaceful people; but family reunions were not very frequent, except for an occasional convivial party. Funerals provided the only opportunity for coming together in state. They thus gained almost an official importance beyond that conferred by the sad occasion which brought us together.

Let me try to recall one of these. It is a dull, cold day. The funeral guests, all a little shy, are gathered together in the small parlour. They are seated round the room, soberly enthroned upon horse-hair and mahogany. The backs of the armchairs by the fire are protected from contact with hair oil by neat crochet antimacassars worked by the ladies of the house.

There were no baked meats, but a few refreshments with consoling properties on the sideboard. The room is pervaded by a strong smell of cigars and the best black rapee. Only a subdued light penetrated through the lowered venetian blinds and drawn lace curtains which fell from above the windows to the floor. The canary suspended in the cage in the window was silenced by the untimely twilight. We had no cretonnes with self-toning art shades in those days. We were content with lace curtains. To us they were often of beautiful design, and while screening the windows allowed a softly diffused light to enter the room.

Old friends are assembled here, a few of whom we only meet at funerals, and all are in deep mourning. The ladies are draped in a prickly kind of crape which sets your teeth on edge when you accidentally brush against it. They wear deeply flounced and bustled dresses, and neat toques or bonnets perched on high coiffures. The gentlemen are dressed in long black frock-coats and wide trousers, while every waistcoat is adorned with gold watch chain and swinging seal. Their necks are protected by high, pointed, white collars, which encroached upon the cheek, and further by a big black bow or tie over a generous expanse of white shirt-front. The chimney-like top-hats with their wide crape bands are placed on the floor beside their chairs.

The conversation is in keeping with the solemn moment. It revives in our minds memories of half-forgotten members of the family, and brings news of others quite unknown to us. Their biblical and sometimes mythological names, such as Seporah, Uncles Matthew and Jonathan, Hester, Dinah, Aunt Martha, and cousins Phœbe and Harriet the twins, sound strange in our young ears. Notes are compared in subdued voices. Family resemblances are traced, much to the confusion of the younger members of the family, who are the principal victims of the research. Family news is exchanged, and the sum total and circumstances of the widely distributed clan are determined for the time being. These will be registered in our minds until the next meeting of this kind, when in the natural course of events they will again have to be revised.

There were a few of these friends whom we only saw in deep mourning and in these solemn surroundings, and we could not avoid the feeling that attending funerals was their life's work. This was particularly the case with an old second or third cousin, a bookbinder by profession. I could not help thinking that he must have been born in mourning, and nursed in black long clothes and bonnet, and that even now he must do a little undertaking as a hobby. I could not imagine him ever to be other than as we always saw him, a funereal and respectable gentleman. He was a stout, rather sleepy and embarrassed man, with a bald, fat forehead and sleek hair. His eyebrows, moustache and short whiskers were all in mourning, as I remember him. Like the other gentlemen he was clad in deep-black clothes, and had, moreover, a wide expanse of dicky beneath his bow. We never quite understood how this dicky was secured, as sometimes it slipped just a little to the side, exposing his

The Funeral Guest

bare chest. Only a peep, you must understand, and not nearly enough to be at all indelicate, but enough to set us wondering.

At last, in a sickly atmosphere of cigars, lilies and warm crape, we shyly followed the deceased to the waiting cortege. The ladies lowered their long dark veils and we took our places in the carriages; for we all went to the funeral. There was no doubt about the hearse; it was a real hearse and deserved the name. It was not one of those rather frivolous and finicking open glass hearses which were beginning to be favoured by the well-to-do, but a sombre and dignified vehicle. It was a square closed-in coach like a great black casket on wheels, with knobs at each corner of the roof, like black chessmen. It was drawn by two fat black horses, crowned with ostrich plumes.

It was all very solemn and grand and a proud moment in our young lives. At a walking pace we progressed down our road, past the blinded windows of our neighbours' houses, martialled by the dignified undertaker himself, on foot, with flowing hatband. Then at a rather brisker pace we passed the shops in the main road, and the crowds who absurdly went on doing ordinary things as though there were no such things as funerals. The cemetery gates were reached at length, and almost at the same time a bell began to toll, as though it was expecting us.

To the melancholy rhythm of the cemetery bell the procession moved slowly along the gravel drive, which was bordered by stone angels weeping at urns, and displaying every other manifestation of stony grief. Here and there we passed vaults, and respectable villa-like mausoleums with little front gardens and the names of the tenants over the entrances. It seemed that knockers and letter-boxes on the front doors would not have been altogether out of place. We wondered who kept the latch keys of these sad little homes of the dead.

As we left the carriages we were surprised and grateful to find awaiting us other friends, whom we were too embarrassed to greet more than formally. We then entered the chapel, and in due order of precedence seated ourselves in the pews. It was a dreary place, and the motif of decoration seemed to be the vanity of all hope and consolation. It had a saddening effect on all of us.

There was another funeral party already in occupation, but as each party kept to its own side of the chapel, and each, with rather studied deliberation, took no notice of the other, it did not matter very much. The clergyman could officiate as quickly over two as over one. He certainly did his best to get it over as soon as possible. He must have been a very busy man, since he polished off the graveside service also in a very summary manner, and then left us, hurriedly hitching up his threadbare surplice, to fulfil another sad appointment.

We lingered for a little time at the graveside, and deciphered the latest inscriptions upon the family gravestone, now ignominiously tilted on its side in the clay. Then, after bidding our last farewells to the departed, we resumed our places in the carriages.

As we returned, our restraint gradually fell away, and in a little time, with a sense of relief, we found ourselves talking in ordinary voices of ordinary things. It came about quite naturally. Even the drivers seemed to breathe again, and to be quite cheerful fellows beneath their professional gloom. After a stop at the Bald Faced Stag, the regular house of call for returning mourners, the restraint was completely banished.

On arriving home the venetian blinds are again drawn up and the canary welcomes the returning afternoon light with a burst of song. The company should now have heard the reading of the will. As I have no recollection of this rite ever having been performed, I must conclude that I was too young to be present at the ceremony, or, what is more likely, that the Robinsons never had anything to leave. Certainly they never left me anything.

CHAPTER SEVEN

Art Students

GREATER enthusiasm than that of the young art student of my student days, it would be difficult to find. His pathetic devotion to his varying ideals and his soaring ambitions are among the finest things I have known. Yet in retrospect, there is something sad in the thought that so many have dropped out or for some reason or other abandoned their ideals, some for lack of means to continue their studies, others because a more remunerative prospect has opened before them, and others again because they have found the limits of their abilities.

I was about fifteen years of age when my parents realized that I should not benefit by staying longer at school, and so I left and joined this gallant band. My father and I had no hesitation in selecting the path I should follow. Not that I had excelled in drawing to any remarkable degree, but that I showed far greater liking for this than for any other pursuit. I did not want to be anything else than an artist. I was a little contemptuous of those of my acquaintance who started life under the restraints of an office. At the same time deep, down in my heart, I secretly envied them the amount of pocket-money they always seemed to possess, and all they could do with it. We made the best of our position, however, and gloried in our comparative poverty and freedom.

First of all I went to an art school in Islington where I met one or two other art students with the same hopeful outlook on life. We worked hard intermittently and talked a lot about art. The vexed questions that cause so much controversy to-day amongst art critics we answered long ago, to our satisfaction at least. Frankly, there was no limit to my ambition. Not that I told myself I should rival Velasquez or Rembrandt, but there was at that stage of my artistic career a pleasing indefiniteness as to my future development. To me as yet anything seemed possible. I flattered myself with the possibilities rather than the probabilities of what was waiting for me in the future.

My ideas of an artist's life were taken from the lives of the great masters which I loved to read. It was only a matter of choosing whether I should paint frescoes in cathedrals and monasteries, or whether I should wander all over the world painting mountain scenery or old cities, and, on an occasional visit to my own country, the woods and fields of England. This last seemed to me the ideal life.

Tom and Charles were following the same profession. At a solemn meeting we decided on the various rôles we should play in the world of art, thus avoiding overlapping and competition. Tom, as a kind of artistic cock of the walk, took upon himself the rôle of Michael Angelo. Charles and I had to be content with those of Raphael and Titian respectively. After a while, with the full approval of the committee of three, I altered my rôle to that of a follower of Claude and Turner.

This amicable arrangement did not prevent us interchanging our rôles at times. I can remember about this time, knocking off a few sketches of a heroic character. "The Triumph of Order over Chaos" was a pet theme of mine, also "Creation" or "The Last Judgment" were subjects that never daunted me. Tom likewise at times did not disdain a landscape and Charles would adopt either of our rôles when required. In this way he discovered a versatility that never left him, bringing fresh surprises to us almost to the end of his life. Charles at the beginning of his artistic career was not quite so fortunately placed as Tom and I. Instead of becoming a whole-time student at the school of art he was apprenticed to a lithographer, and only attended the class in the evening. In the long run this handicap, if such it was, does not seem to have affected his work. Whether he would have benefited by a more academic training it would be difficult to say. Perhaps it would have checked his delightful freedom and his most original fancy.

It was a little difficult to descend from these ambitious flights to the comparative drudgery of drawing a vase, a cube, and a cone arranged on a board, or the plaster cast of a piece of ornament from the Ghiberti Gates at Florence. We lived in a world of plaster of Paris. The studio was crowded with plaster casts of the Discobolus, busts of Roman emperors and empresses, the Venus de Medici, the head and shoulders of the Hermes of Praxiteles and fragments of many other well-known examples of the plastic arts. The walls were hung with casts of hands and feet of famous statues and with architectural fragments. We became so accustomed to drawing fragments, that we were inclined to prefer figures in a state of mutilation to the commonplace examples with a normal number of limbs. The plaster often became chipped and being unwashable it had to be painted periodically. In this way much of the modelling in course of time became smoothed out.

We tackled this unpromising material with a zeal which, at this distance of time, I cannot help admiring, though I may regret that so much youthful enthusiasm should have been expended in this manner. Doubtless we derived some good from this method of teaching, but we had little else for years when so much of a more life-like interest was awaiting our study. Fortunately we had opportunities to cultivate our imagination. A great incentive to this was the monthly Sketch Club.

The students of the school constituted a cheerful family united by similar ideals and aspirations. The one discordant element was old Captain Fripp, who, whenever his ship anchored in the port of London, put in a few days at the school. There was no nonsense about the Captain; he wasn't bothered about art, technique and such trash, but did a bit of solid seamanlike work, making copies in oils from a book of views of the Isle of Wight. These were to be given to his friends, we supposed, or perhaps they decorated the walls of his cabin. He was a taciturn man and worked in a little room all alone. He had no patience with the younger fry, whose work he considered trivial and their liveliness mere frivolity, instead of the result of a higher training and a superior intellectual outlook as we imagined them to be. Another old seaman, a messmate of his, would sometimes call on him and be wrapt in admiration of his work. They would then retire for an hour or so and the Captain would return alone, much refreshed, and resume his work on a view of the promenade at Ryde.

Miss Belfry

I cannot write of this period of my student life at the Islington School of Art without recalling memories of William Coe. Some at least of the old students will remember him and his beautiful work. His design, his colour, and his sense of the beauties of light together with his vital imagination were the qualities of his work which most aroused our admiration. I can only indistinctly see him in my memory as one always in failing health, yet without the melancholy and apprehension of an invalid. His delightful sense of humour never left him. So lighthearted and hopeful was he, that a life of glorious artistic enterprise might have been before him instead of his untimely death. Not the least of his endearing qualities to us, the younger students, was his kindly interest in our progress and his willingness to impart to us what knowledge he had acquired and we could assimilate. He became in time almost a legend with us, and left an influence for the good which I hope has never departed.

Not to be forgotten was the heroic Miss Belfry, who had spent the greater part of her life following the profession of music, in which I was told she had gained considerable distinction. Suddenly, at the age of fifty, or thereabouts she discovered that she had mistaken her vocation. Wiry and indomitable, with a shock of iron grey hair standing erect on her head, she devoted every ounce of her energy to the pursuit of art. She always carried about with her, besides a mahl stick for use at a moment's notice, an eye bath. With this, at frequent intervals, she swabbed her eyes, thus enabling them to resist the strain put upon them in these strenuous endeavours to make up for the lost years. She was an egoist, certainly, so were we all, but heroes and heroines in the cause of art, as we understood it, for all that. Then there was Ernest Prater glowing with good health and fresh from triumphs at the military tournament. He varied his and our studies by giving us lessons in single-stick.

Old Mr. Pol was another of my fellow heroes. He had retired after many years of faithful service in some Government appointment. Did he seek a life of well-earned ease in which he could prepare himself for his latter end? Not a bit of it. He wisely decided to begin life anew and become

Mr. Pol

an art student. Not one of us could excel him in enthusiasm and interest in his new profession. In spirit he was as young as any of us and in many ways as simple and naïve. Sometimes his second boyhood would disappear and a quixotic gravity possess him. In this mood he would moralize to us with old-fashioned wisdom. More worldly wise though we imagined ourselves to be, his transparent simplicity and sincerity were apparent even to our young minds and never caused a smile.

Even tired Mr. Merle was, when quite awake, a devotee to art, though admittedly this was not very often. He had a love for painting still life. Now and again his constitutional weariness would overtake him at work and he would fall asleep. Sometimes he would awaken with a start, to find that the cherries that he had been painting had unaccountably been removed or changed into grapes. He rubbed his eyes and heroically worked on, only half conscious that something was amiss.

I was not the only one who, recently relieved from the irksome restraints of school life, revelled in my newly found freedom. I must here recall my old friend Percy Billinghurst who was contemporary with me. We were great friends and later were to share a studio for many months. He will be remembered affectionately by old students of this school and of the Royal Academy Schools. We, the younger students more particularly, were like so many students before and since, quite conventional in our unconventionality. We almost regarded ourselves as of a superior caste to that of the ordinary youth. He perhaps was constrained to observe the accepted conventions of society—to be always well-dressed, with hair brushed and combed, to be at the office punctually every morning, to take a mere pittance of holidays, a fortnight in summer and a few days off at stated times during the year. We were above all this, we were on top of the world and life held out infinite possibilities for our exuberant selves. We pitied these poor fellows with their cramping responsibilities. I have lived to envy them many things and to admire them in more.

So much exuberance required a restraining hand, and for this we had nothing more formidable than the presence of little Miss Thomson—the art mistress of the school. She had a bird-like manner and exercised her authority in the kindest way. At times a harmless and humorous sarcasm with only the faintest suggestion of vinegar would give point to some mild rebuke. I am sure that her gentle sway was far more respected than that of a stricter disciplinarian would have been. She worked hard on her own account, painting flowers, and she supervised our earlier studies. Her teaching was very careful and conscientious.

She bowed down, as did most of the lady students, in a half romantic awe before the master who visited us at frequent intervals during the week. I knew little of his work, but he was a real artist if ever there was one. He couldn't be mistaken for anything else. He wore a black velvet coat and artistic tie. His head was that of a pale young Moses adorned with a long silky beard, moustache and waving hair. The finishing touch to this artistic personality was the gold-rimmed monocle which continually dropped from his eye and was replaced as he took a broader or closer view of your drawing. His name was Henri Bosdet and he was of French descent which was subtly betrayed now and then. The ladies pronounced his name in the French manner and addressed him as Mr. Bo-day. We, out of perversity and to his annoyance, called him Mr. Bozzdett, preferring an English pronunciation.

One of the aims of this institution was to prepare students for the Royal Academy Schools. Admission to these was obtained by studentships which were competed for twice a year. Those of us who intended to follow this course, after gaining a certain proficiency, continued our studies at the British Museum. We now bade adieu to plaster of Paris, of which we were rather tired. Too much plaster, after a while, has a tendency to enter the soul and check its expansion. We now entered upon the marble stage of our art education, and glutted ourselves with antique. We had to conduct ourselves with an almost religious decorum in these solemn galleries of the British Museum, which echoed loudly even to a pencil falling on the floor. In the solemn presence of Rameses the Great, of Osiris, of Zeus, and the Principal Librarian who stalked through this Temple of Gods and Heroes, we endeavoured to suppress our native light-heartedness. I did not always find this possible.

After lunch one afternoon, I was returning to my work whistling gaily " Little Dolly Daydream the Pride of Idaho " under the very eyes of Diana of Ephesus. I was walking briskly round the base of the statue, when I almost fell into the arms of the Principal Librarian. Nothing could exceed the wrath of this High Priest of the Temple at my sacrilege. It was only at the intercession of the attendant, who could vouch for my industry and good character, that the threat of instant ostracism was withdrawn. Crestfallen, I returned to my work between rows of frowning Roman emperors and empresses, only gaining a little encouragement from the knowing glance of a laughing faun.

At the Museum we met many other hopeful young students from art schools in different parts of London. They also were preparing drawings for the Royal Academy Schools. Success in these efforts seemed to us to be very much a matter of chance. I have known students of very great promise try time after time and be rejected. The Royal Academy Schools presented to them the only means of continuing their studies satisfactorily. On the other hand some, who had no pretentions to real ability and for whom it could have been only a matter of indifference whether they succeeded or not, easily obtained admittance to the schools. I do not altogether attribute this to want of judgment on the part of the Royal Academicians of the time, but to the utter inadequacy of the tests applied. Whatever the cause the results were sometimes tragic. Since then the whole system has been altered and many heartbreaking disappointments avoided.

Long before the time of which I am writing, no age limit was imposed. I can still remember the legend of an old lady who had been trying for many years unsuccessfully to gain admission to the Schools. It was said that in her early youth she had been crossed in love and had taken to art in despair. Every six months since then she had been sending up the required batch of drawings and only desisted when the age limit was made. After this I was told she took to copying old masters in the National Gallery, and found peace at last.

Artistic enthusiasm at the British Museum was not confined to candidates for admission to the Royal Academy Schools. I can remember one eccentric student who was conspicuous for his zeal. It may be considered that in his case it was rather madly applied, but no one can deny that it deserved admiration. He was employed in an office and could only spare a quarter of an hour each day for studying the antique. Wild of eye, he would burst into the Museum at the allotted time; with considerable clatter he would set up his easel, and for ten minutes or a quarter of an hour work frantically. When his time was up, he hurriedly packed and was gone as quickly as he came. It took him many months to finish his drawing, but it was to his credit that this was finally accomplished.

Our paths crossed again in later years. I was walking along a country lane not far from London one summer evening and saw his well-known figure seated at an easel. He was painting the sunset. Three years later I happened to be walking in the same lane and sure enough, there he was still at work on the same picture. He had been working on it ever since in brief moments of spare time. He was always cheerful and hopeful and invited criticism which he never resented however severe it was. He might still have been working on the same sunset at the close of day, but, alas, his own day is over and the picture will never be completed.

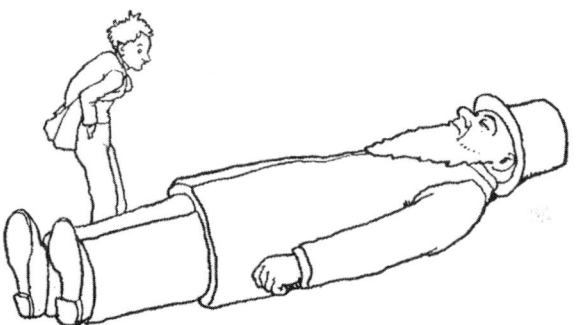

Whom it was meant to represent I could never discover

I considered myself fortunate enough in becoming an Academy student after my second effort. The system of teaching I found in the schools could not have greatly changed since the days of Sir Joshua Reynolds. Although this was not the original home of the schools which he founded, his spirit was certainly about in the place. Perhaps at night when all the students had gone home and the place was in darkness, he wandered up and down the long corridor from which the studios opened, with a volume of his *Discourses* under his arm. Or he may have haunted the great yard that ran down the side of Burlington House. I would sometimes wander into this yard out of curiosity. It was a busy place on sending-in day. What attracted me to this spot was a colossal statue of a frock-coated, top-hatted respectable gentleman with an umbrella. It was lying neglected on its back by a wall. Whom it was meant to represent, I could never discover. Whoever he was, there he lay doing nothing in particular, a monstrous monument of respectability. It was some satisfaction to see so gross an idol biting the dust. I could cry with the prophet, " Arise ye chosen people, Baal is fallen." It was said that the statue had been sent to the annual exhibition many years before and been rejected. Rumour further had it that the sculptor not being able to afford to fetch it away, had fled the country leaving no address. Instead he left a problem that the combined wisdom of the Royal Academicians found some difficulty in solving.

I had now been drawing antiques for the last five or six years, and found to my dismay that I was to continue to do so. I do not question the value that drawing from the antique may have for the art student, but too much time was given to working up the modelling with delicate chalk stipples, a tedious and laborious process. One young lady so excelled in this that her drawing of Hercules struggling with the Hydra rivalled the finest crochet work. However, these studies were, to my great joy, varied with painting and drawing from life. My attendance at the schools was never very regular, and I had few opportunities of entering into the social life of the students or making new friendships. Amongst those of my contemporaries, who in varying degrees have since become famous were Charles Sims, Derwent Wood and Montford, the sculptors, G. E. Stampa and Lewis Baumer, both regular contributors to *Punch*, Byam Shaw, Frank O. Salisbury and Harold Speed. Of these several have passed away.

The necessity to earn my living was now becoming more and more urgent, and my all too brief academic career came to an end.

CHAPTER EIGHT

The Landscape Painter

I WAS still leading an untrammelled existence and was jealous of the least infringement on my liberty. I was faithful as far as possible to my ideal of an artist's life. I can justly say that I was not mercenary and was innocent of any desire to become wealthy. If riches came my way with no effort on my part to obtain them, that was another matter. No doubt as an artist I should know the right way to use them. It was the peculiar privilege of an artist to have a clearer insight into the real value of such dross, and many other things too, so I held. I now felt that to preserve my valued freedom and spirit of independence I could not for much longer be wholly dependent upon my parents. They had ungrudgingly supported me as long as their slender means warranted them to do so. Although anxious for me to earn my living, they were even prepared to strain further their resources on my behalf. They were not much more worldly and provident than I proved to be. I now determined, if it were possible, to make this sacrifice unnecessary. Tom and Charles were both earning their living and this made my position more difficult to endure.

The problem now confronting me was complicated by the number of ways by which it seemed possible to solve it. It was only on closer examination and after many tentative experiments that the difficulties they nearly all presented were evident to me. Portrait painting promised a lucrative living, but so few people wanted their portraits painted, at any rate by me. Church decoration would have been congenial work, but nearly all the churches were already decorated. Those who commissioned work for the decoration of theatres or houses or for the illustration of books and magazines were as unresponsive to my overtures as the buyers of subject pictures or landscapes. I was equally unsuccessful in convincing scene painters of the value of the help I could give them. At last I realized that I should have to take one of these branches of my profession and heroically persevere with it in spite of every discouragement and temptation to turn aside.

For the immediate purpose I had in view, it must be admitted my final choice was not a wise one. Even before the day when Tom, Charles and I had undertaken our different rôles in art, I had a love for the life of a landscape painter or such as I fondly imagined it to be. It still possessed me and I resolved to gain my independence by success in this congenial occupation. My idea of the life of a landscape painter was to live in the open air and in lonely communion with nature. To be hardened to all weathers, heat, cold and all climates. To be equally at home in raging storms and under the dazzling sun of the desert. To be unfettered by the restraints and conventions of life in town. This was the way to live. The where might be anywhere. Sometimes, perhaps, in the Swiss Alps or the Himalayan Mountains and Tibet. At other times my wanderings might take me to Greece, to Rome or to Egypt and back again to the Norfolk Broads. Greenland would surely be visited, and hence some dashing sketching expedition to the polar regions was not without the bounds of the landscape painter's wide possibilities. All these and many other wonderful places would be taken in my stride.

The ideal landscape painter

I was an incorrigible day-dreamer, and in my foolish infatuation, I pictured myself tramping the country roads without a care and returning from some painting expedition in the Austrian Alps or by the Bay of Baiae. My clothes were worn almost to rags, but by Turner and by Constable, what did that matter to one who despised the vanity of the neatly clothed townsman and held as naught his approval! My face was a rich brown by exposure to the weather and my hair was blowing in the wind. Upon my back was strapped my paintbox, some few superb works of art, destined for the National Gallery via the Royal Academy, and my scanty baggage. With what admiration and envy was I greeted on my return by those few intellectuals who—— and so on.

As a matter of fact it did not quite work out like this. I found that my daydreams were apt to lead me on in this manner and leave me in the end, as La Belle Dame sans Merci left that other wretched wight—on the cold hillside. Greece, Rome and the Himalayas were a long way off, so I wisely decided to begin on some place nearer home. These more remote fields could be attacked at a later time. The scene I selected for my operations was the wide neighbourhood of Hampstead Heath, Parliament Hill Fields and Highgate Ponds, which had the advantage of being within walking distance of my home.

We now lived in Stroud Green, a suburb in the North of London, which covered the once green hill we knew as the Hog's Back. Our house was still farther from the original starting-point of the Heath Robinsons. This outward trend had begun before we were born. My father first saw the glorious light of London somewhere in the neighbourhood of the Pentonville Road. Since then by successive moves he had at last reached Stroud

Green. At so slow a pace it would take a long time to reach the country, but I am convinced that this was the attraction that almost without our knowledge was drawing us away from town.

This trend I was to continue later by trekking to Pinner and then farther still to Cranleigh in Surrey. Was there a trace of vagrancy in the Heaths and Robinsons, the former generations of whom so determinedly migrated from the country to the town? Perhaps in the days before King Alfred the Great some Heathrigg or Robinwolf started the slow journey on the other side of the North Sea. If so, it must be confessed that the journey since has not called for any too heroic effort and has been continued in easy stages. Mayhap, to break its monotony, some Willibald Heathrigg-Robinwolf would draw a white horse or two on the downs. Though varying fortunes may have been met with, there have been happy stopping-places by the way.

The Hampstead Heath at the time to which I have now brought my story, was not surrounded by suburbs as it is to-day. From its borders fields with farms stretched far away to Finchley and Harrow. Though not the untouched countryside it was in the days when Constable painted it, or Mrs. Bardell visited the Spaniards Inn, it was still very beautiful. It is true there was no lichen on the trees, few wild flowers, and the wear and tear of the London holiday-maker were already breaking up the old order of nature that can never be mended. Let us hope that the end is still far off, but it surely approaches and at last we must make that fixed compromise with nature which is sometimes so beautifully achieved in the formal parks and gardens of town.

The heath is approached from the north of London by Hampstead Lane. It was not then a tarred motor road but a winding country lane of the colour of ivory, and sometimes of gold. Every morning I walked along this highway to my work on the heath. I can see myself whatever the weather, a rather unkempt figure uncomfortably burdened with the equipment of a landscape painter. I am afraid I did not resemble the heroic figure of my daydreams, but I tramped on bravely enough for all that, my mind perhaps pursuing some quixotic folly the while.

After a spring of cold showers, it was a beautiful summer that I spent painting on Hampstead Heath. I became one of a curious little group of landscape painters. They were a picturesque band and such as I have never met with since. They were stray artists and, belonging to no particular school, were mostly self-taught. Art galleries rarely saw their work and collectors ignored it. Nevertheless a good painting was sometimes produced. One of our band was an old Scotsman whom we looked up to as the master of the group, rather in virtue of his years than the merits of his work. He was very poor and lived the vagrant life of a hedge artist, moving from one sketching ground to another. Apparently he sold every picture he painted but at such small prices that he may truly be said to have led a hand-to-mouth existence. Fortunately he had not a large laundry bill to meet, but there were his lodging, food and drink to be paid for, and the last was no small article in his expenditure. Every picture he painted was to meet a bill, and most of his financial dealings were transacted in a canvas currency. At times, without warning, he would mysteriously disappear for two or three weeks at a time. And then one morning we would recognize his old bent figure and well-worn coat among the furze bushes in some sunny hollow of the heath. He was back again working off some debt.

In the early morning we had the heath to ourselves and for a few short hours it seemed to return to its prime, to the days when London was far away. The light seemed purer, and the air as it gradually lost its coolness was filled with the rich warm smell of the furze. The morning progressed, and one of a little gang of derelicts from London who loafed about the heath would saunter up. Seating himself on the grass at my side he would engage me in conversation. There was some indefinable suggestion of the vagabond about these hangers-on. If they did not get their living by their wits, I should be puzzled to say how they managed. In any case they made a poor job of it. I was advised not to let my paintbox or other belongings lie beyond my reach while they were about. I do not think they regarded me as their prey. I believe they were taking a little time off from their jobs and were on a holiday. One is apt to forget that even those who live by their wits need a change sometimes, when they can banish from their minds all thoughts of petty larceny and the anxieties aroused by the vigilance of the police.

The doctor

Very different from these was a conversational doctor who spread himself over the heath at this time. He, like Micawber, whom he resembled in appearance, was waiting for something to turn up. How he lost his practice if he ever had one I do not know. Perhaps he was wanting in a good bedside manner, which requires, one would suppose, not only the gift of conversation but also that of listening attentively and sympathetically. This latter gift was certainly not possessed by the doctor of Hampstead Heath. Whatever the cause of his unemployment, he had plenty of time to spare and spent it in talking to anyone who would listen to him. There was some mystery about him, which he was inclined to foster. But he allowed a hint to escape, as it were accidentally, that he was connected with a well-known county family.

He was portly, and imposing in a Micawber way, and a faint suggestion of shabbiness did not detract from his gentility. In a grand manner he was interested in the lower orders and tolerated them with a generous condescension which he flatteringly extended to me. He was always interested in any signs of intelligence that they displayed, and was on the whole genuinely hopeful of humanity. He was sometimes accompanied by his wife, a gentle and worried lady who idolized him.

As the day wore on the changing light would compel me to move my pitch. I would leave the wilder heath on the northern side of the Spaniards Road and set up my easel in the yet peaceful country of the Vale of Health. Later still in the day, the tea gardens in the Vale will be filled with a noisy crowd of youths, young children and their parents.

The late afternoon sun shines through the pollarded willow trees which grow all around the tea gardens. It flings dazzling patches of light, almost too bright for the eyes, indiscriminately amongst the joyful crowd. Here one falls upon a white tablecloth and the cups and saucers arranged upon one

They carry large trays loaded with cakes

of the rustic wooden tables, or it partly illumines a mother holding a baby with one hand while pouring out tea with the other. She is surrounded closely by clamouring children. Some are in shadow, but one is revealed with pudgy arm outstretched towards the cakes, the bread and butter and fruit. Another beam of light may catch the brilliantly dyed ostrich feather on the broad-brimmed hat of a girl. Where the sun cannot penetrate, all is cool green shadow. The gaudily painted swings creak and rattle as they move up and down with their noisy occupants. The perspiring white aproned women, who wait at the tables, run frantically backwards and forwards through sunlight and shadow. They carry in their buxom arms large trays loaded with teapots and jugs, with plates stacked with bread and butter and strawberry jam and slices of currant cake. The gilded roundabout blares and snorts cheerful holiday tunes from its leather lungs—"Daisy, Daisy, give me your answer true" or "The Man that broke the bank at Monte Carlo". Through the leaves of the willow trees it can be seen revolving in barbaric splendour of blue and red and gold, and beyond, like brilliant turquoise jewels set in the green, glimpses of the lake reflecting the afternoon sky.

The crowds of children, tired at last, gradually disperse with their parents, their aunts and their uncles. The heath is left to the lovers. It is a long while since I ate my frugal lunch and now real hunger besets me. I shoulder my bundle and trudge homewards. A delightful weariness overtakes me, my face is tingling with sunburn and the strong sweet air of the heath. So, one of the many happy days of my life is brought to a close.

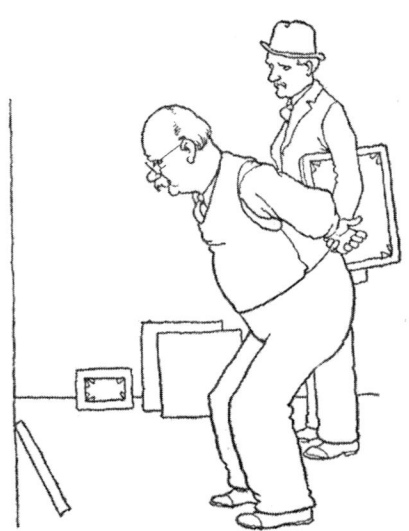

My hopes began to rise

My Hampstead Heath period, though productive of much happiness and good health to me, did not bring me appreciably nearer to the end I had in view. I seemed as far from earning my living at the end of my Hampstead summer as at the beginning. I took some paintings to a dealer. I think his shop was in the Balls Pond Road. He was quite a pleasant man. He greeted me warmly and examined my work very critically and silently. So long did he remain gazing through half-closed eyes and with his head on one side, that my hopes began to rise. Surely, thought I, if my work was of no interest at all to him he would have known this at once. At length, he began to rub his chin thoughtfully and shake his head slowly.

"How long have you been painting?" he asked.

"About four or five years," I replied.

"Have you ever sold a painting before?" he queried.

"No," was my brief answer.

He then asked: "Have you got to depend upon your own earnings for a living?"

I explained to him that this was certainly how I was placed.

"Well in that case I should try something else," he said kindly. He then helped me to tie up my canvases again, and shaking hands, bade me good-bye in a very friendly manner. He stood at the door of his shop in his shirt sleeves eyeing me curiously as I departed down the road. I was at that age when disappointments do not wound too deeply. I soon found consolation for this rebuff. After all, thought I, what can a man who lives in the Balls Pond Road know of art?

Of all the paintings and sketches I made on the heath, I only sold one. This was bought by the mother of my friend Fred Smith. The sale of this enabled me to spend a holiday with my friend, for which kindly purpose I have more than a suspicion that the purchase was made. It is always exhilarating to be with Fred Smith, but particularly on a holiday. He had so many enthusiasms, and he held them so strongly that it was impossible to be with him for long without sharing them. He took a generous bite out of life and digested it with enjoyment. We went to Lelant in Cornwall where we shared our quarters, a little Cornish cottage, with his brother-in-law Francis Black, R.B.A. The latter, who always took a friendly interest in me and introduced me to Alfred East, R.A., was painting in that neighbourhood and advised me about my work.

I have been to Lelant in Cornwall more than once in later years. I have walked along the inlet to see the sea coming in over the harbour bar. I have revisited Carbis Bay and St. Ives, but I failed to recapture the joy of this holiday of long ago. All was changed, or was I changed and less alive to the glamour and romance of this light-drenched land than in that happy time? Here, so the legend told us, Saint Paul had wandered, and long forgotten peoples had left their altars and graves to arouse our wonder. I only sold one painting in all that year but never have I had such generous payment.

CHAPTER NINE

Bread and Butter

ALTHOUGH my first art transaction had such satisfactory results, I had to admit that it was not of a nature to encourage the hope of my being a successful landscape painter. To sell a painting to a friend, who may have been prejudiced in your favour or at the least anxious to do you a kindness, was good as far as it went. It was a different matter to persuade unknown buyers of the advisability of purchasing my work; buyers who had no such friendly prejudices, and certainly had no particular wish to do me a kindness.

Charles's apprenticeship had now for some time come to an end. Tom and he were following what was almost a tradition in the family Robinson. They were making drawings, and selling them too, for reproduction in books and magazines. This was in the days when Aubrey Beardsley, who exercised an influence over all of us, was in his prime; when Sime had begun to harrow us with his weird conceptions, and when Charles illustrated that delightful edition of *A Child's Garden of Verses* by Robert Louis Stevenson. I was now of necessity drawn into this field of work, and not unwillingly. I thought I saw in it great opportunities, not only for the development of what was best in an artist, even a landscape painter, but for earning a living. Ever since the days when we amused ourselves with drawing on slates, we had been in the habit of filling sketch books with slight drawings prompted by our fancy or imagination, as much for the fun of it as for any bearing it would have on our future as artists. I believe that this habit played a greater part in our artistic careers, wrongly or rightly, than the more academic training we received at our art schools. It was this thread that I now took up and tried to adapt to the end I had in view. I worked in my father's studio at Danes Inn in the Strand. This was, for my father, conveniently near to the editorial offices of the *Penny Illustrated Paper*. Danes Inn was a dreary place after Hampstead Heath. It was as cold as stone, of which material the two tall rows of houses which composed it were mainly built. They were separated by a courtyard paved also with stone.

My father occupied a suite of two rooms at the top of No. 1. It was approached by a very wide circular stairway with an iron railing to deter anyone so disposed from throwing themselves on to the pavement below. A stale smell of old dinners pervaded the place and belied the otherwise prison-like character of the building. The depressed spirit was not greatly refreshed on entering my father's door. The front room in which we worked overlooked the courtyard, and the air was dry and smelt of dust. The walls were hung with one or two old charts, and I can remember an ancient macabre print representing, in allegorical form, the Spirit of " Gout " gnawing the foot of some victim of this complaint. The dried body of some poor puss of long ago was suspended near the fireplace and grinned with fiendish glee at an old blunderbuss on the wall. This was rather gruesome and the less understandable because the Robinsons were always fond of their cats. In retrospect, a long procession of them passes before me. Boss, Nelson, Wolsey, Peter, Barty, George Barker, Sheringham, Fred and Saturday Morning— the last, an immense veteran of thirteen years, who still survives and dreams away his declining years by the fireside. Here he waits resignedly for his passing to some feline paradise where he will join all the old Robinson cats. Was this poor blackened mummy all that remained of some long since deceased Robinson pet? On the mantleshelf was one of my father's ship models, now a wreck in a sea of dust; a sad reminder of the days when my father wished to be a sailor.

The smaller room was usually sub-let to a wood engraver or another artist. In the old days, long before I worked here, it was occupied by a staff of three or four engravers. I can see them now as I saw them on one dark and foggy morning. They were all bent low over their work. Glass globes filled with water increased the light that came from the green-shaded lamps. Each engraver wore a protruding eyeglass like a watchmaker's glass fixed to one eye. This he brought as close as possible to the wood block, for it was the finest work they were executing. The wood blocks were poised on round leather pads like buns, which could be revolved at will. It was fascinating to watch the engravers as they toiled quietly on in the warm air of the room. After each cut was made in the wood, the graver was brought up to the lips or moustache to clear the tool. One poor man in this little group of workers was suffering from consumption. So little was known in those days of the most elementary principles of Hygiene that the engravers all worked closely together unperturbed.

Tom and Charles had already served some time in Danes Inn. Our young spirits were not too depressed by our surroundings. I have no doubt now that we gained much from my father's more businesslike knowledge, though we were inclined at the time to be rather supercilious about it. I worked hard at drawings, humorous and otherwise, whose inspiration was mainly derived from my imagination. By gradually adding to my collection and eliminating the least satisfactory of my efforts, I at last gathered together a set of drawings, with which I thought myself justified in beginning my campaign against the publishers and art editors. They were quite unaware of the deeply laid schemes to overcome them, and, I think, were taken aback

Those chilly mornings: ingenious devices fitted in the most up-to-date flats and maisonettes in Golders Green

by the boldness of the attack. Armed with my portfolio, my first sally was directed against their western wing, and I called upon John Lane in Vigo Street, W., and another publisher, whose name I forget. Failing here, in the West, but still undeterred, I concentrated on the enemy's centre which lay across the district of Covent Garden. On the edge of this, in Leicester Square, Grant Richards was strongly entrenched. In Bedford Street, were Heinemann and the castle of the venerable Dent. Although at a later date he was to succumb and commission me to illustrate some books for him, I now only received a paternal blessing.

It was at Dents', but some time later, I first met Frank Swinnerton, who has since become so well-known as a writer. He was then very young and used to be seated in the outer office at a closed-in desk, defending the approach to the reverend presence of the publisher. It was encouraging to meet one so friendly as Frank Swinnerton in the enemy's camp, at these anxious moments. Tom and Charles, who had been here on similar adventures, also felt his kindly interest in the Robinsons. He was much younger than we, but we were all more or less at the beginning of a struggle, which has, perhaps, not ended for all of us, but which has brought him such well-merited success. It has been a great pleasure to me in recent years to illustrate some of his writings. I now proceeded to attack Isbisters'—a publishing house which I believe has long since disappeared. I met here the kindly William Canton, the author of *The Child's Book of Saints* and *The Invisible Playmate*. A fine edition of the former was illustrated by my brother Tom and published by Dent. I was cheered on my way by William Canton's interest in my work, an interest which he did not disguise. I was soon to make some illustrations for *Good Words*. Very immature they were, as I am sure he realized; nevertheless, I received generous encouragement which I gratefully remember.

Neither George Bell & Sons, the book publishers, nor Newnes nor Pearson's were to fall to me as yet, but their time was to come. I was now warming to my task and with renewed vigour resolved to outflank the enemy's eastern wing. On my way I had a slight skirmish with the publishing house of David Nutt in the "Strand". Some time after they were to publish one of the first books I ever illustrated. This was *The Giant Crab* written by W. H. D. Rouse. It was a collection of stories for children based on Indian folklore. They were so naïvely and humorously written, I have seldom had a subject to illustrate that made a stronger appeal to me. As with most of the books I illustrated in these early days, I would like to illustrate them all over again. Alfred Nutt was then the representative of the house. He was a tall thin man with the air of a scholar and who, it seemed, should have been writing books rather than selling them. The narrow pass of Paternoster Row and its immediate neighbourhood were now invaded. Hodder & Stoughton, the Religious Tract Society, Warne's, Cassell's, and Partridge's were all subjected in turn to a kind of artistic barrage.

Partridge's, amongst their other publishing activities, dealt in the sale of clichés, that is of blocks reproducing drawings that had already been published, a kind of second-hand transactions. I was once asked to convert a print from one of these, a diagrammatic reproduction of some fishes from a book on natural history, to an illustration for a fairy story. I had to paint over the indication numbers and draw in a baby seated comfortably among the fishes. The fishes were all very stiff and in profile, but the result was considered satisfactory. It certainly appeared to be economical for I suppose they only had to pay for the baby, the price for which was not high although the baby was a fat one. The fishes, if they had to be paid for at all, they could have had at second-hand rates. These and other publishing houses put up a good defence, but at last a breach was made. To my great joy I sold a drawing to Cassell's for *Little Folks*. Other triumphs soon rewarded my persistency. Work began to come to me instead of my having to hunt for it. It was a satisfaction to be sought for, but I regretted those long tramps and the sense of adventure that accompanied them, the hope with which I set out in the morning and the joy when success rewarded me.

It now became necessary for me to take a farther step in my great adventure and to find a studio of my own. My old friend and artist comrade P. J. Billinghurst was in the same position, and we resolved to take a studio together. We discovered one which seemed to meet our requirements both as to rent and accommodation, in Howland Street, a turning off the Tottenham Court Road. Our landlady was Madame Schmidt, a stout red-faced lady who was partly Nordic and partly Hebrew. There were many other tenants in the house evidently of the same strain. Besides ourselves, the only one of the community who was of British stock was Murdoch, a Scottish artist, who lived in a cavelike studio deep down in the basement of the house. He started life as a hosier in some obscure town or village in Scotland. He felt the call and, with a truly heroic courage, threw away the means of a livelihood and came to London to paint pictures. How he subsisted I could never discover, but I believe that Mme. Schmidt was good to him. He lived entirely for his work, which, as I remember it, was sometimes obscurely allegorical and rather wild. His gestures were slow and gentle and his eyes were alight with enthusiasm. One felt that he ought to have been a genius—perhaps he was.

Our own studio was a small square room like a box with a top light.

"*Bombay*": *an illustration from* "*A Song of the English*" (*Hodder & Stoughton*)

It was constructed of match-boarding and had no side windows. It was built over a stable, but how a stable could be in such a position was a mystery to us. There was no possible entrance to it, that we could discover, in the neighbourhood. Nevertheless a stable was undoubtedly there. We could hear the horses stamping below. We should not have objected to this very much had the stable been clean, but unfortunately this was not the case. Now and again an overpowering smell of stale stable would steal through the planks of the floor and pervade the room. To-day I wonder, when I remember how long we endured this, yet we worked hard for some months in our little box which we had furnished as neatly as our means would allow.

In a studio not far away in this grubby and Bohemian world, dwelt O. M. Badcock. He was a fellow student of ours at the Royal Academy Schools. He began his training under Professor Brown at the Westminster Art School.

I cannot pretend to understand a character so unusual and seemingly so wilful as that of my friend Badcock. His work was exceptionally good and good without apparent effort. He had encouragement from masters whose reputation should have given it great value. I believe he loved his work and he appeared to have every opportunity that could be wished for developing his abilities, opportunities which we envied him. Unaccountably, he threw all away, and after a time never touched a brush. It is easy enough to call it laziness, but I do not think this the solution of so sad a riddle. Perhaps it was despair of attaining some excellence he felt to be beyond him. He has been for many years far away in British Columbia. He is still consistent in his continued interest in art, but alas, also in his complete abandonment of any intention to excel in it. He has written some good verse which has been published in many journals in Canada and the United States. He had a sense of humour all his own and he was best of all as a boon companion in the mild orgies in which we sometimes indulged.

Less difficult to understand in these spare times was a poor artist who lived in another studio near to us. While we sympathized with his poverty, we pitied his meanness. After work he would put the unused paint on his palette back into the tubes, or try to do so. This we could not understand, no poverty could excuse it. We swore that we would sooner live and die in debt than be guilty of such parsimony. As we were often in debt ourselves, we felt justified in taking up this strong attitude. Although our pockets were not always well filled, we had at least a generous outlook on life. I was once holding forth with big-hearted gestures in praise of artists; I maintained that rarely could you find an artist unwilling to help another in his difficulties. Some little time after my audience, all deeply impressed, had left me, there was a gentle knock at the door and my parsimonious friend looked in. " I say, Robinson, could you lend me two bob for a couple of days?" he asked. I thought this rather unkind.

After a few months the ghostly steeds of Howland Street drove us away to seek another studio. This we found in, or rather on, a house in Gower Street. Here we were more healthily situated, in a wooden erection on the roof of the house and open to all the winds. It was good to be up here in a storm. The walls shook and creaked but our trim built craft was taut and seaworthy. At these times, we would picture ourselves blown from our moorings and sailing gaily over London. We would alight on the roof of some publishing house—on Dent's or Nutt's or Bell's and attack the publisher from above. Covering him with a revolver we would demand a commission to illustrate the whole of Shakespeare's works, the *Encyclopædia Britannica*, and a few little things like that. And not merely with pen and ink vignettes,

An illustration to " Rabelais "

(See page 123)

but with full-page colour drawings plentifully scattered throughout the works.

There were other studios in the house, one of which was occupied by James Aumonier, the landscape painter, whose picture " Sheep Washing in Sussex " was bought by the Chantrey Bequest. I had, and still have an admiration for his work, and was proud to have a studio in the same house with him. He was brother to William Aumonier the sculptor and decorative artist who was the father of the late Stacy Aumonier. William Aumonier was a decorative artist in more than one sense—and a picturesque figure as he walked down the Tottenham Court Road. He was, as I remember him — a square and florid man, not very tall, and with a most cheerful mien. His large leonine head was crowned with a mass of dark hair and a broad-brimmed black hat. On one occasion, I am told, when he was travelling on a crowded bus, the conductor regarded him with considerable awe and after taking his fare announced to the astonished passengers that they were travelling with the great Lord Tennyson, the Poet Laureate.

And sailing gaily over London

I was now twenty-four years of age and was at least beginning to earn my living. In the year 1900 I illustrated the poems of Edgar Allan Poe for the Endymion series of Poets published by George Bell & Sons. This was the most serious task of the kind that I had as yet undertaken and the first in which there was not some element of humour. In looking to-day at the work of these early years, I must admit that much of it was immature, and over ambitious. I often overestimated my abilities. For this reason every drawing was a fresh adventure into new countries in which I found some advantage for myself and openings for further adventures. Although confined within such narrow limits, where there were no dragons to slay nor barren wildernesses or mountains to cross, it was for me a life of joyful enterprise.

At this period I became conscious that I was being haunted by a strange little genius. He was not altogether unfamiliar to me. I fancy that he had haunted me almost unrecognized for many years. Now for some inscrutable reason he made himself more and more evident. Where he came from I cannot tell. At some time in his existence he must have wandered long in Alice's Wonderland. The only book he seems to have read was Gilbert's *Bab Ballads*, but even these he did not read as we read them; he took them quite seriously as we do " Shakespeare " and *Smiles' Self Help* and *Eric, or Little by Little*. He was sincerity itself, and he had the simplicity of a child combined with the wisdom of old father William. No mortal could compare with him for ingenuity and inventiveness. He could do wonderful things with a piece of knotted string. There was one thing he lacked and that was a sense of humour; perhaps this was not a loss, for strangely enough it made him all the more humorous. It seemed wrong, however, to laugh at one so earnest, so guileless and free from cynicism, but at times he was irresistible. Fortunately, he was far too busy to care whether I laughed or not. My good genius in many ways, he introduced me to new friends and revived old friendships that were almost forgotten. He tempted me along a path which ran quite independently of that followed by my more serious work. He first

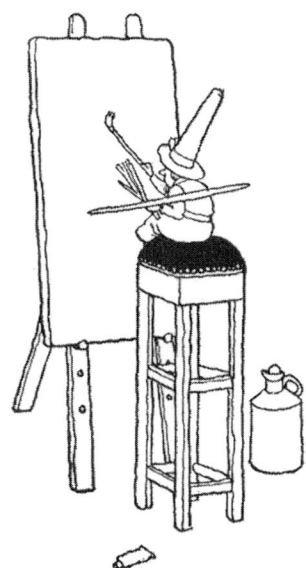
My little daemon

Haunted by a strange little genius

came to visible life as " Uncle Lubin ", whose life and adventures I wrote and illustrated about this time.

One of the first to whom Uncle Lubin introduced me was that enterprising publisher Grant Richards, who published the " Adventures " in the year 1900. It was through this introduction too, that I was commissioned to illustrate *The Works of Rabelais* also published by Grant Richards about two years later. It is a testimony to the publisher's enterprise, at any rate, that he should commission the author of " Uncle Lubin " to illustrate " Rabelais ". " Uncle Lubin " was also responsible for my introduction to the eccentric T. W. H. Crosland, the author of *The Unspeakable Scot* and other satirical works. These created much surprise and indignation as well as amusement in their day. Bitter and scathing as his writing may have been, I always remember him as a genial friend and as one who gave me great encouragement, at a time when this was needed. He occupied the responsible position of publisher's reader to Grant Richards; whether he considered it one of the duties of his position, I do not know, but we

My good genius introduced me to new friends

would often walk across to the Café de l'Europe, after I had taken some drawings to the office, and indulge in amusing conversation with others who gathered there to meet him. To such strange and varied companionship did " Uncle Lubin " introduce me.

Some time after this, I became involved in law proceedings. A publisher, for whom I had recently illustrated a book, became bankrupt. The work, however, was issued by the creditors subsequent to the bankruptcy. I imagined that in this case I was entitled to the payment originally agreed upon with the publisher. I, or rather my counsel, argued that I should not be classed as an ordinary creditor. We were wrong, it seemed, and I lost my case. It would have been a greater loss had I not already received a part of the payment for the work. But to one whose only contact with the law had been as a juryman, its majesty was rather alarming. One soon gets used to it, I am told, but fortunately I have never had the necessity to do so. I found, as I usually do in vexatious circumstances, some consolation in fanciful imaginings. It was a busy time at the courts, and pictures of extreme congestion and ways of dealing with it arose before me. I saw the benches with two judges, and twenty-four jurymen were empanelled in order to get through the work in half the time. Many other strange thoughts passed across my mind, some of which I treasured and at a later date embodied in a drawing.

CHAPTER TEN

Uncle Lubin

MY good genius, now in the guise of Uncle Lubin, not content with furthering my professional aims, began to interest himself in my private life and decided it was time I married. My future wife and I had already decided this for ourselves, having been engaged to be married for some little while, but unfortunately we could not afford to do so. This was no obstacle to Uncle Lubin, who, in an underhand way, brought about the possibility of a fulfilment of our wishes. I received a mysterious letter from one who signed himself Chas. Ed. Potter of Toronto. He informed me that he had been reading *The Adventures of Uncle Lubin*, which had convinced him that I was the artist to illustrate some advertisements he was writing. He further asked me to make an appointment with him at an hotel, the name of which I had never heard before. I believe it was called " Tranter's Hotel ".

I had so often heard of the nefarious dealings of unscrupulous tricksters from the other side of the Atlantic, that I felt this was a case for using caution. I made an appointment and duly called at the hotel. I found it to be a very homely and old-fashioned house tucked away in some quiet square near to St. Paul's Cathedral. I was shown into his room, a snug little bed-sitting-room, and introduced myself to Chas. Ed. Potter. I cannot remember what I expected to see, but he was not at all of the gangster type; on the contrary he was the most amiable little man, who beamed at me in a friendly way through a pair of gold-rimmed glasses. I could easily imagine that Uncle Lubin and he got on very well together. Nevertheless I remained on my guard; for you never know what wiles may be practised to take advantage of an innocent artist.

While agreeing to do the drawings, I did so only on condition that I received cash payment for each one as it was delivered. Cash in those days meant solid gold. In effect, I was to deliver a drawing with one hand while he was to pay into the other its worth in gold. Chas. Ed. Potter appeared to see nothing unusual in these stipulations and readily agreed to them, though I fancy a twinkle of amusement escaped through the gold-rimmed glasses.

Every two or three days for the next few weeks I called at the hotel with my drawings. One of us seated on a chair and the other on the bed, we then discussed and planned the next set. I was soon ashamed of my suspicions and my stipulations lost all meaning. It was, however, so satisfactory to return from my visits with a little pile of gold in my pocket, that I could not remove the conditions I had imposed.

So at last we were able to be married. I have to thank Uncle Lubin not only for his help in this important event in my life, but for a great friendship which began in a little bed-sitting-room in Tranter's Hotel by St. Paul's Cathedral many years ago.

The advertisements were for the Lamson Paragon Supply Co. Ltd., with whom I now entered into a long and happy association. Chas. Ed. Potter returned to Toronto, where he is now engaged in overseas trade promotion and many other activities, in which good will is the inspiration. Later J. M. Evans, now the Managing Director of Lamson Paragon, came to me with an introduction from him. Advertising, I am told, is a serious science, and I have no doubt it is, but to me as an illustrator it has always been great fun. Perhaps at times I saw too much fun in it and needed a restraining hand. Such mad vagaries as those included in the drawing entitled " Some new and ingenious methods of advertising " would arise to my mind. However, my friend J. M. Evans and I collaborated together happily for years, and I like to think he enjoyed it as much as I did.

Unfortunately, Uncle Lubin was not a best-seller, but I have reason to believe that he endeared himself to those children in whose library he was placed. In the few copies of the original edition that I have seen in late years, the line drawings have often been coloured by some childish hand. Though the colours are gaudy, I flatter myself that this was a sign of loving appreciation. I have often been asked by parents, who in their own childhood have lived with Uncle Lubin, where they could buy a copy of his " Adventures " for their children. Children's books receive so much wear and tear that they rarely survive one generation. Having some knowledge of the use of string, I have been able to keep my copy intact. I have even heard of a hand-basket being used to contain the dismembered pages of an old and well-worn copy.

H. G. Wells in one of his earlier novels remarked that children regard Uncle Lubin as a rare good thing. I think that this expressed the appeal that Uncle Lubin was intended to make to children. For them he was rare and good; to be admired and loved rather than to be laughed at. The smiles are left for the parents who buy the book. This childish attitude towards my drawings is well expressed in the following letter I received from an unknown correspondent written in a scrawling hand:

DEAR MR. ROBINSON,

I do so love your pictures that I want to call my hedgehog after you. May I please.

NOEL MONTAGUE.

New and ingenious methods of advertising

I have always been pleased that my lighter drawings appealed to H. G. Wells. I was interested too, that one who took such a serious view of life should be so alive to the humours of these imaginary little people, childlike and serious, and their earnest activities. At a later date than that to which I have now arrived in the story of my life, I received the following letters from him:

LITTLE EASTON RECTORY, *New Year's Eve, '14.*
DUNMOW.

DEAR SIR,

It may amuse you to know that you are adored in this home. I have been ill all this Christmas-time and frightfully bored and the one thing I have wanted is a big album of your absurd beautiful drawings to turn over. Now my wife has just raided the Sketch office for back numbers with you in it and I am turning over lots of you. You give me a peculiar pleasure of the mind like nothing else in the world. I can feel myself getting better.

Do you know Buntingford? I discovered the place some year or so ago and in it there are perhaps half a dozen houses of which you might have been architect. I motor over at times simply to look at them. I hope you will go on drawing for endless years.

Yours very gratefully,

H. G. WELLS.
Not the Revd.

EASTON GLEBE, DUNMOW.

DEAR HEATH ROBINSON,

I am a pleased and happy man this day. Half the pictures I've already got, cut out from the periodicals in which I found them. One of these days, when the sun shines again, I shall raid Moss Lane in a little automobile and take you off to see Heath-Robinson-ville, which is Buntingford.

And then I shall bring you on here for a week-end.

Yours ever,

H. G. WELLS.

Whatever success these drawings may have had was not only due to the fantastic machinery and devices, and to the absurd situations, but to the style in which they were drawn. This was designed to imply that the artist had complete belief in what he was drawing. He was seeing no joke in the matter, in fact he was part of the joke. For this purpose, a rather severe style was used, in which everything was laboriously and clearly defined. There could be no doubt, mystery, or mere suggestion about something in which you implicitly believed, and of this belief it was necessary to persuade the spectator. At the slightest hint that the artist was amused, the delicate fabric of humour would fade away. I do not pretend that this end was always achieved, but I was so far successful as to be frequently identified personally with my drawings.

I was imagined by some people to be a kind of ingenious mad-hatter, wandering around absent-mindedly, with my pockets full of knotted string, nails and pegs of wood, ready to invent anything at a moment's notice. I was once interviewed by a hopeful young journalist. When he entered the house, he glanced suspiciously at the lock on the front door, expecting, I suppose, to find some ingenious device for opening and shutting it. His eyes wandered inquiringly round the hall, and I think he was disappointed that there were no pullies and mechanical devices for doing things. Seated in my studio he took out his notebook and opened fire.

"Now Mr. Robinson, where do you get your ideas? Do you dream of them or what?"

These are always difficult questions to answer so I mumbled a non-committal reply.

"Now, Mr. Robinson, where do you get your ideas?"

"Of course you were trained as an engineer?" he queried with his head on one side.

I could only answer "No."

He seemed a little incredulous of this.

"All your inventions would work, you know," he said with an encouraging smile. I was doubtful of this, but I grinned as though I thought it quite likely. He now continued brightly:

"No doubt the house is full of your devices, for bringing coal up to the studio, for hanging out the washing: and tell me about all the contraptions that I am sure you have fitted up for communicating from one room to another and all that sort of thing: you know you must be a useful man to have in the house."

I could not honestly agree with this so I smiled again without definitely committing myself one way or another. For some time he fired off these questions at me and I am afraid he received no more satisfactory answers. However, I do not think it mattered very much, for a few days afterwards an article appeared, which told me many things about myself which I had not realized before. If the readers of the journal were really interested in the matter, they could now find out exactly what I was like.

The success of these drawings was not instantaneous; some art editors were doubtful of the wisdom of publishing them. It would not be fair to accuse them of a want of a sense of humour because they could not smile at my work. A sense of humour is such a personal matter. A drawing of mine would appeal strongly to one person while to another the same drawing would be without meaning.

In these early days of my campaign as a comic draughtsman, I once submitted some drawings to an art editor. On arriving at the publishing offices I entered by a door labelled " Enquiries ". I explained the object of my visit to a young lady seated at a desk on the other side of a counter. My portfolio was taken from me, and I was politely shown into the Waiting Room. This was a glass-framed cubicle, furnished lightly with a chair and a table on which were placed a blotting-pad, a dry ink bottle and a pen-tray with no pens. By the side of the table was a waste-paper basket in which were a few torn galley sheets, and one of the walls was decorated with a calendar. I took a seat as requested, and the door was closed upon me. This flimsy cell in which I was confined at least performed its function as a waiting-room. I waited anxiously for so long that I began to wonder if I had been forgotten. The air was filled with a strong smell of printer's ink, and in the distance could be heard the rumbling rhythm of printing machines at work.

At last the door opened and a boy in uniform appeared.

" Mr. Robinson ? " he queried.

I assured him that he was not mistaken, and I was ushered into the presence of the art editor. I found this great man very closely examining my drawings which were spread out before him. After inviting me to be seated, he said.

" These are very interesting drawings, Mr. Robinson, but———"

At this moment a clerk entered with a proof sheet, and a consultation took place. When this matter was disposed of he resumed, smiling apologetically:

" As I was about to say Mr. Robinson, these drawings are very interesting and show careful work, but what we are looking for is something really funny, you understand, something to make our readers laugh."

" But," I remonstrated, " they are meant to be funny, they are———"

The telephone bell rang. Having arranged an appointment for to-morrow's lunch, he turned to me again with a smile, and I continued:

" They are intended to make people laugh."

He appeared to be doubtful of this.

The Reproach

"Then do you ever do any what you would call serious work?" he asked.

"Oh yes," I replied.

"Well," he said, "if this work is humorous, your serious work must be very serious indeed."

"It is," I retorted.

But here the conversation was again cut off by the ringing of the telephone bell. While he was engaged with this, I seized the opportunity, withdrew my drawings from before him, and myself from his office.

I was disappointed. I looked again and saw no humour in the work. I wondered how I could have been so hopeful. This rebuff almost paralysed my efforts to proceed. At a later time, I took the same drawings to another publishing house with different results. The art editor did not attempt to conceal his amusement. I once more regarded these drawings hopefully and was encouraged to go on in the same vein. In this way I was helped to gather together an audience which has been faithful and helpful to me ever since.

The late Clement Shorter, at that time editor of *The Tatler*, published some of my earlier drawings, but I think he was always a little doubtful about them. He eventually gave up publishing them altogether. Bruce Ingram, the enterprising editor of *The Sketch*, was very encouraging. It was largely due to him that I was fairly launched on my career as a humorous artist. I also had early recognition from *The Bystander* and *The Strand Magazine*.

It was at the offices of the *Strand Magazine* that I first met Sydney Boot, the son of W. H. J. Boot, R.I., at that time the distinguished art editor of that journal. W. H. J. Boot had himself done much illustrating for *The Illustrated London News* and the old *Black and White*. The public, publishers and illustrators as well, are indebted to him as being the pioneer of artistic art editing. His son James Sydney Boot followed his father as art editor of *The Strand* but in 1919 relinquished this position, and joined A. E. Johnson and his brother E. W. Boot in their artists' agency.

At the outbreak of war, Sydney Boot tried heroically but unsuccessfully to enlist for foreign service. He even tried to get the War Office to send out a battalion of "Old Crocks"—a suggestion which was refused. His persistency was only rewarded when the age limit was extended and he joined the Artists' Rifles. Few men have so successfully combined friendship with business. From the early days when I took my drawings to him at *The Strand Magazine* I was always pleased to feel that he had a kindly interest in me and my work. It seemed that he extended this kindness to all he dealt with and little enough to himself. I, and many another artist too, lost a friend when he died.

Spring cleaning in Highgate Woods

It was his father who commissioned my brother Tom to illustrate that famous series of articles on London by George R. Sims to be published in the *Strand Magazine*. These two innocents used to wander all over the town in search of subjects for articles and illustrations. Opium Dens, Thieves' Kitchens and other picturesque hells were visited, but the wanderers came through unscathed. Strangely enough the first series of drawings I made for the *Strand Magazine* was a crime series. Unlike George R. Sims and Tom, I did not seek out crime, but had to evolve it from my inner consciousness. This might be imagined to be a dangerous experiment, but I also came through unscathed as far as I know. It is true, I did not have to scour Bethnal Green or haunt the Ratcliffe Highway to find the Kind-Eyed Winkle Pilferer of Paddington Green, one of my favourite criminals, but found him much nearer home and arrested him without any trouble in the studio.

It will be obvious that the little daemon who haunted me had for some time abandoned the guise of Uncle Lubin. Not content

An expert in the detection of crime

with rescuing children from bag birds, sea serpents and other monsters, he was now seeking a wider field. He was making a heroic attempt to adapt himself to the times. He became in turn an expert in hunting and fishing, in British industries and manufactures, an inventor, a sportsman and an expert in the detection of crime. One of his first efforts in this wider field, was " the gentle art of catching things ", a series I carried out for the *Sketch* under his inspiration. The series included such perilous occupations as " Tickling for the Bandicoot in New South Wales ", " Trapping Whelks by the Caucasian Sea ", and " Noosing Wild Cats by the Kyles of Bute ".

This was followed by " Great British Industries ". " Stiltonizing Cheese in the Stockyards of Cheddar " aroused interest but some doubt as to the practicability of the method. On the other hand, the mechanism in " The Pea-splitting Shed of a Soup Factory " was considered to be quite practicable. Its only drawback was that, dealing with each pea individually, it would take too long to split a peck of peas. It was not thought to be a profitable pro-

"*The King of Troy's Army*": *An illustration*

position and was never adopted. My little prompter was like that. He maintained that the first consideration in the process was the splitting of the pea. This was true enough as far as it went. He thought that if this was done satisfactorily it was merely trivial to worry about other considerations such as the time taken in the operation.

"Little Games for the Holidays" and "British Sports and Pastimes" made a strong appeal to the sportsmanlike instinct of the race. The game of "Bouncing the Beecham" was reproduced and played in India. The costumes of the players and the umpires were all carefully copied from my drawing. I have not heard that the game ever became a national sport. One of the pet theories of my rather persistent taskmaster was that all sport should serve some useful purpose. "Moths," said he, "are the bane of the housewife." He made many suggestions for their extermination but that embodied in the drawing entitled "Trapping the Clothes Moth in the Wilds of Idaho" seemed to me to be the most feasible.

from " Bill the Minder "

My drawings were frequently carried out as life-size models. A flying ship from one of my drawings was seen at a water carnival on Lake Saranac. The report does not say that it actually flew, but, as my guiding spirit would say, " It ought to have done so." One gratifying sign of the appreciation of my drawings was the number of suggestions I received from all over the world. It was good to feel that I had so many friends, for friends indeed they were; few things unite people so intimately as a kindred sense of humour.

One of the most serious rôles played by my guiding spirit was that of an expert in the detection of crime. He imagined himself to be a superior kind of Arsène Lupin or Sherlock Holmes. My part was that of his Watson. At any rate, he dictated to me rather forcefully, and prompted me to carry out a series of drawings for the *Sketch* entitled " Tec Tactics ". Although it may be difficult to imagine these Tactics assisting in the detection of crime, yet, as my mentor was careful to point out, there was no logical reason why they should not do so. He was nothing if not logical.

In the year 1912 I wrote and illustrated *Bill the Minder*, a more ambitious undertaking than *The Adventures of Uncle Lubin*. It was composed for older children than the readers of the earlier work, yet it was inspired by the same spirit. It was concerned first of all with Bill, a minder of children, the Virtuous Boadicea, one of his young charges, and the King of Troy. The last was not of the house of Priam, but a member of a later and hitherto unknown dynasty. He had lost his throne through the machinations of some evilly disposed ministers. Bill, Boadicea, and the other children of Crispin, the mushroom gatherer, formed the nucleus of an army which undertook to restore the good old monarch to his throne. The army set out on its journey, meeting with strange adventures, and, as it progressed, its numbers were increased by many strange and interesting people it met by the way. These included " The Sicilian Charwoman ", " The Ancient Mariner ", " The Lost Grocer ", " The Respectable Gentleman ", " The Real Soldier ", and " The Mixed Triplets ". Each had a story to tell to beguile the way, and all contributed finally to the restoration of the old king to his throne.

An interesting instance of reproducing my lighter work in model form occurred about this time. I designed a scene in a Revue at the old Alhambra Theatre of Variety entitled *Kill that Fly*. It was composed and arranged by the late George Grossmith, junior, in collaboration with André Charlot. The scene was called " Epsom Ups and Downs " as imagined by Mr. Ascot Heath Robinson. The back cloth consisted of a picture of a Heath Robinson racecourse. This wound in extravagant serpentine curves over the ups and downs. The foreground was occupied by a model of my well-known Starting Machine. This worked quite successfully and proved that it was possible by mechanical means to start all of the horses at one time. I am not a racing man, but I can well understand that this is necessary in horseraces.

Amongst the crowd Mr. Ascot Heath Robinson meandered gracefully, a not very sportsmanlike but still an interesting and picturesque figure. Not being an actor, I could not appear in person on the stage, and the part was cleverly played by Mr. René Koval, an actor practised in such impersonations. Great pains were taken that the resemblance should be as close as possible. We would stand side by side, while my counterpart was made up to resemble me. So exact was the resemblance, that I trembled to think of the great confidence I was reposing in my double. The criminal possibilities were obvious, but my trust was never abused.

I was invited to attend a rehearsal. Having been warned that my scene might come on at any time during the day, I went as early as possible in the morning in order not to miss it. I had never been to a theatre in these circumstances and found it difficult to become used to the unfamiliar aspect

Myself and my " double " (played by Mr. René Koval)

f everything. The dark auditorium, the covered seats, actors and actresses clothed in their rehearsing costumes seated in the stalls, and ordinary non-acting people walking on the stage, where they seemed equally out of place, were all rather bewildering. I was seated in the stalls, while I watched the turns as they rehearsed their parts over and over again. I was expecting and hoping that at any moment my scene might come on. It was all so delightfully casual, with frequent pauses: everyone was friendly and nobody seemed to be in a hurry.

At lunch time, we all retired to another part of the building, where a good lunch awaited us. We all sat down together, actors and actresses, George Grossmith and André Charlot, and had a jolly and sociable time. I was glad to find in George Grossmith one who had a sympathetic appreciation of my efforts at humour. He was such a master of this himself. He was so vital and enthusiastic that it was inspiring to work with him. Both he and André Charlot provided me with every opportunity to make my scene a success, to which they largely contributed by their help and management. When the meal was over we strolled back to the theatre and the rehearsal resumed its leisurely course. At the close of a long and restful day my scene came on. Rehearsals I am told are often strenuous and tiring to all who take part in them. Perhaps it was because I was only an onlooker, but my memories of this one are of a happy and peaceful day in the comfortable stalls of the old Alhambra.

CHAPTER ELEVEN

Big Business

ONE of the difficulties I find in tracing my line of life, arises from the fact that it has many branches, a characteristic, I believe, not confined to my own line of life. While following one, I must leave others behind and from time to time go back to pick up the dropped threads of my story. I have never yet discovered which is the main line and which its tributaries and have tried to follow all without favour. This has compelled me to lead a dual existence and as much thought had to be given to my lighter work as to my more serious drawings. One day I might be illustrating Kipling's *A Song of the English* or a Shakespeare play and the next would find me at work explaining the Gentle Art of Catching something. It was always a mental effort to adapt myself to these changes, but with the elasticity of my early days, it was not too difficult.

Would not have considered the proposal

This variety in my work was not a problem to me alone. I remember a visit to my studio of one interested in my lighter work. Among other drawings, I showed him an illustration to a poem by Edgar Allan Poe. He was puzzled and very disappointed at the absence of machinery. Thinking that he was expected to be amused, in an embarrassed manner he forced a laugh which was not at all convincing. My name became so closely associated with humorous work, and a byword for a certain kind of absurdity, that my signature on more serious drawings was, I admit, disconcerting: I had never been asked to submit rough sketches for decorating the interior of St. Paul's Cathedral, but were I capable of doing so with the most beautiful frescoes, I am afraid that the Dean and Chapter would not have considered the proposal for this reason. Even without my signature, there would have been a temptation to imagine in some biblical Patriarch or Prophet a remote resemblance to a figure seen in a different connexion elsewhere in my work.

I was once approached with a view to making some drawings for an illustrated edition of the Bible. I believe I had at least one advocate on the committee who presided over this undertaking, but I am afraid the rest were scandalized at the suggestion and we did not proceed with the negotiations.

In the year 1899 I was at work on my illustrations to the Poems of Edgar Allan Poe to be published by George Bell and Sons in their Endymion series of Poets. I was gratified to have the illustrations of a book in this series, made famous by the illustrations of such artists as Anning Bell and Garth Jones. My dealings were with Mr. Edward Bell, a fitting representative of this old publishing house with a great tradition consistently maintained for a high standard of publication. He appeared to be a scholar and was always affable and very encouraging.

As I have mentioned before, I often wish that I had the opportunity to illustrate these poems again. At the time I had neither the power nor the experience to take full advantage of the scope they provide. I console myself with the reflection that perhaps other illustrators have the same thought on looking at their earlier work. It is not often that opportunities occur for illustrating the same work twice, though I have been fortunate enough to illustrate one three times. This was *Hans Andersen's Fairy Stories*. The first time was for a cheap reprint published in the year 1897. As may be expected the work for this was very crude. The second time was for an edition published by J. M. Dent in the year 1902. This was illustrated by Tom, Charles, and myself in collaboration. The last time I illustrated these stories was for an edition published by Constable in the year 1913. As far as my drawings were concerned, this was certainly the best and was, I hope, enhanced by the many colour illustrations. These three books show well what development I had made as a book illustrator in that period.

Wood engraving was no longer used for the reproduction of illustrations, or only very rarely: the zinc line block necessitated a style which Aubrey Beardsley made perfect. I do not mean that his genius depended on anything so mechanical as a photographic process of reproduction, but that being almost the only means of reproducing drawings in those days, the work was necessarily influenced by the peculiar opportunities it provided for the use of pure line and also by its limitations. Aubrey Beardsley, Sime, Walter Crane, Anning Bell, my brother Charles, Garth Jones and many others were well-known members of the school of illustrators that arose from these conditions. The influence that all of these had upon me is reflected in my illustrations to Edgar Allan Poe's Poems.

I envied the success my brothers had gained. Charles had become famous with his illustrations to *A Child's Garden of Verses* published by John Lane in 1896. This was followed by the illustration of other books of a similar character written by H. D. Lowry, Gabriel Setoun, I. Henry Wallis and Walter Gerald.

" The Girl who trod on the Loaf"
An illustration from " Hans Andersen's Fairy Tales " (Constable)

Tom had illustrated among other books *The Sentimental Journey* and *Cranford*, both published by Bliss, Sands & Co. in the years 1897 and 1901 respectively. I do not think these classics have ever been more beautifully illustrated. He was influenced not so much by the decorative line work of the British School as by the earlier illustrators, and even more by that great Spanish artist and master of line, Vierge.

Inspired by this genial influence

Charles's wedding soon followed his early prosperity. It took place in the year 1897. He was one of those happy and gifted people who inevitably attract many friends. He became the centre of an admiring group of artists, authors, and even publishers. Many of these attended the feast; John Lane, H. D. Lowry, Walter Gerald, Evelyn Sharp and the Rev. Percy Dearmer were among the many guests. The last named conducted the ceremony at the church. It could not be called a society wedding, but it was a great marriage feast for all that. It took place on a sunny day in April when the almond blossom was out and thoughts of weddings and betrothals were in the air. Even the older guests were inspired by this genial influence, by the lovely spring afternoon, the light dresses, the smiling faces, the flowers and the champagne. They laughingly recalled their own wedding days and long years of happiness since.

I remember one old gentleman so overcome by the memories of his own married joys, that he loudly proclaimed with animated gestures: "I have been married for sixty years and never have I said an unkind word to my wife." It is true his wife was not there to corroborate his statement, but we gladly took his word for it, drank his health and cheered him heartily. After this outburst, he sat back and beamed with gratification. Towards the evening when the bride and bridegroom had departed, the wedding feast became more boisterous and tended to overflow and spread beyond the house. The

Beamed with gratification

next morning, festivities were continued on a modified scale, but at last they gradually died down, and the full realization dawned upon us that Charles was married. This event marked an important stage in the history of the Robinson family. It was the first wedding in the younger generation.

I now illustrated *The Talking Thrush* by W. H. D. Rouse, and made many drawings for a popular edition of *The Arabian Nights* published in serial form by Constable. This was followed by my illustrations for an edition of *Don Quixote* especially adapted for young people, and then by my contributions for the Hans Andersen to which Tom and Charles also contributed. Both of these works were published by J. M. Dent in about the year 1902. This work of mine though still at times immature, began to show a diversion from the work I did under the influence of Beardsley and the other illustrators of his time. The illustration of Don Quixote, for whom I had and still have a great love, demanded a different treatment, a treatment which came more and more natural to me. It found its greatest opportunities in *The Works of Rabelais* which I was now to illustrate. I like to think that this change in my work accompanied a change in my outlook on life. At the least it was more personal and derived its inspiration, not so much from the work of other artists, as from the subject I was illustrating.

Don Quixote attracted me as do all wanderers, from Herodotus to George Borrow. I do not include in these, those great men who travel to the ends of the earth and benefit mankind by their scientific discoveries, but those who wander along the country roads seeking other things. Don Quixote was the Prince of these. Such were Christian in *The Pilgrim's Progress*, St. Francis d'Assisi and many another pilgrim. It was this love of mine that made " Uncle Lubin " and " The King of Troy " wander along their narrower roads. It was this love, too, that makes me enjoy so much a day's walk in the country. There must be no certain goal but that sense of mild adventure to be found on an unknown road. Yes, there was more than a trace of vagrancy in the Heath Robinsons.

My work was becoming more varied, and involved much clerical labour as well as business direction. The question of copyright, foreign and serial rights now arose to complicate my affairs, and cause unwelcome distraction. As these worries increased, I began to find that I had neither the time nor the inclination and perhaps not the necessary experience to deal with them satisfactorily. On the advice of Rudolph Bezier, I decided to place all these cares upon the broad shoulders of A. E. Johnson, the Artists' Agent. The terms " Agent " and " Client " barely describe the friendly relationship that has since existed between us. In a series of books under the general title *Brush, Pen, and Pencil* which he wrote on the art of some well-known illustrators, he included one on my work. I was encouraged by his criticism of my drawings, but I do not think that he imagined I should agree with the last words of the book. " The fact is Heath Robinson has never grown up, and for everybody's amusement, let us hope he never will." At that time I

"*Master Peter*": *An illustration from* "*Don Quixote*" (*Dent*)

considered myself very grown up indeed; an opinion since modified.

Ernest W. Boot on his return from Germany where he had spent over four years in prison camps, now became a partner with A. E. Johnson in the Agency. In 1919, they were joined by James Sydney Boot after he had been invalided from the army. This partnership was able to work in a wide field, and so cover the varied activities of such artists as myself.

Ernest Boot had the unhappy experience of being arrested in Germany before the outbreak of war. He and some companions, all members of the Artists' Rifles, were on a walking tour in the Black Forest on their way to Switzerland. On 2nd August, 1914, two days before the declaration, they were arrested at a little village called Braulingen. After extensive examination they were sent to the prison Kreisgefängniss at Baden. They were next confined in the Plötzenzee prison, Moabit, Berlin, where they spent some weeks in bug-infested cells. Finally, they were interned in the civilian concentration camp at Ruhleben. Here they remained until the close of the war. The justice of their claim against the German Government for illegal arrest was eventually admitted. The case was heard before the International Court held in London after the war under the presidency of M. Morel, the International Jurist. Compensation was awarded to each of the party. But what could compensate for the misery endured and more than four years taken from a young man's life?

At this time, I became a member of the London Sketch Club. It consisted of a group of artists, who met every Friday evening in the winter season and made sketches. After this a hot meal of a very substantial quality was provided followed by music and various entertainments. When I joined there were many members who have since become famous. These included Frank Reynolds, H. M. Bateman, Dudley Hardy, De la Bere, Edmund Dulac, Sheringham, John Hassall, Lawson Wood, Bert Thomas and Ernest Moore. A few of the members were painters, but they were mostly magazine and book illustrators, poster artists, cartoonists and humorous artists. There were also many lay members, amongst whom were representatives of other professions. They used to assemble after the work was done on Friday evening, and many of them being professional entertainers, made valuable contributions to the evening's programme. For the artists, these meetings provided opportunities not always to be found in their everyday work. Undeterred by the opinion of anyone other than our fellow-artists, we gave a free rein to our fancies and imagination. Since those early days, they have had many distinguished members, amongst whom may be numbered the Great George Parlby, my brother Charles, Albert Toft, Alfred Leete, Fred Taylor, Barribal and Tom Downey.

That the London Sketch Club satisfied a real want amongst the younger artists is evident from its present prosperity. With the exception of a few, the members now belong almost entirely to a new generation and the traditions are held as strongly as in the days when I joined about thirty years ago.

In the first decade of the century, there began to appear that de luxe series of books to which Arthur Rackham and Edmund Dulac made such fine contributions. The appearance of these books was partly due to the development of the three-colour process of reproduction. Unfortunately, this method could only be used on a certain kind of paper that was impossible for the rest of the book. Consequently the colour pictures had to be stuck in, making the book a scrapbook. This was not true book-making, but they were nevertheless handsome volumes.

I was commissioned by Hodder & Stoughton to illustrate *Twelfth Night* to be published in this form. The work was a joy to me from beginning to end; my drawings were designed to give a free illustration of the drama. I am afraid that at times I have not resisted its many temptations to make a picture irrespective of its value as an illustration. But on the whole I tried to preserve the atmosphere of the play as I felt it. The philosophic clown appealed to me all through the work and I endeavoured to insinuate something of his philosophy into the drawings. The art of the book illustrator, as I understood it, did not consist solely in literally illustrating the incidents. His relationship to the work he was treating was much the same as that freer one adopted by a musical composer towards his subject. This play, and the fact that the illustrations were to be in colour, gave me such opportunities as I had not enjoyed before.

The next important task I undertook, was the illustration of an edition of Rudyard Kipling's *A Song of the English* to be published by Hodder & Stoughton in the year 1908. It became necessary for me to meet the author and discuss the proposed book with him. For this purpose, I travelled down to Burwash where he lived at that time. This was an excursion I shall always remember. I was met at Heathfield and journeyed thence in a motor-car. There were few cars on the road in those days and this in itself was a joyful experience as we drove through the pleasant Sussex lanes. Bateman's, the house at Burwash, where Rudyard Kipling lived, was a fine old building with stone mullioned windows. It was in the midst of wind-blown Sussex country. There was a faint smell of the sea in the air wafted across the few miles of country from the shore where

> The Coastwise lights of England watch the ships of England go.

It was a fitting setting in which to find the author of *A Song of the English*.

" Come up, come in from Eastward": An illustration from " A Song of the English"

He met and entertained me with a quiet affability, which speedily removed the shyness I felt at first in his presence. Before long I was quite at home with him. His own knowledge of illustration gave him an appreciation of the artist's point of view. While making suggestions, he realized that the illustrator must have as free a hand as possible. His sympathetic understanding of my part in the undertaking made me feel that I was consulting with a brother artist. I spent a happy and for me a helpful day. It was a great inspiration for the work I had in hand to be in such close association with the author's interesting personality. I am always glad to remember that he was satisfied with my illustrations to his book. This was followed by another Kipling volume, *Collected Verse*, which was published by Doubleday Page & Co. of New York. This had a wider range of subject than *A Song of the English* and was consequently more difficult to illustrate. The Canadian National Gallery bought one of the originals, entitled " The Three Decker ". This was a great encouragement to me.

In 1913, I illustrated *Hans Andersen's Fairy Stories* for the third time. It is interesting to bear in mind that a great number of our fairy stories are derived from European folklore. In their original forms, they were not intended for children. Some of them were very terrifying. The Grimms used them freely, removing from them as much as possible, though not always successfully, their frightening characteristics.

Hans Andersen and Perrault do not appear to have relied upon these sources nearly as much, if at all. Most of Hans Andersen's stories at any rate seem to have originated in his own mind, and have no suggestion of the macabre. It is this happier tone which I have tried to reproduce in my drawings. There are, however, certain traditions in connexion with the illustration of fairy stories, which cannot be ignored. Gnomes and fairies, at least in all European countries, have a family resemblance. An artist cannot invent an entirely new kind of gnome. Perhaps it is this that has convinced many children both young and old that fairies really exist.

The illustration of classics is much governed by tradition. Sometimes this has been created in recent years. Sir John Tenniel created traditional forms for Alice, the Mad Hatter and the Duchess. To every dweller in Wonderland he gave a shape that the illustrator may not depart from. Dickens illustrations also depend to a certain extent upon his early illustrators, such as Phiz, for their types. It is true that these have developed and grown to a ripe growth in the drawings of later artists such as Fred Barnard, but their figures as we see them have evolved from the types set by the early interpreters of Charles Dickens. They have become like Micawber, Pecksniff, Falstaff and Alice, more and more real and recognizable as the immortal companions of mankind. Shakespeare had to wait centuries for a satisfactory illustrator, but Sir John Gilbert's Falstaff makes him visible to us for all time.

Even Sir John Gilbert's accepted version of Falstaff is said to be not entirely his own creation but the portrait of a well-known actor of the past. He no doubt, adopted traditions that may have been handed down from the day of Shakespeare, gradually taking more and more definite form. It seems that an artist only plays a part in his creations. He focuses and passes on what was already in the universal heart of the race. Mankind and Michael Angelo painted " The Last Judgment ".

Every new book to be illustrated brought with it its own problems. The Kipling books, Hans Andersen and *Twelfth Night* had to be considered from widely different points of view. The last was seen through a golden haze of Elizabethan romance; the Kipling subjects in the colder and whiter light of modern times. My edition of *A Midsummer-Night's Dream* was published in 1914, soon after the outbreak of the war. Fortunately at the time I was making the drawings there was no hint of the terrible catastrophe that was so soon to overtake us.

One of the designs for "A Midsummer-Night's Dream" (Constable)

The old Greek stories of the Wedding of Theseus and Hippolyta; of Pyramus and Thisbe and of life in Ancient Athens as seen through English eyes bewitched me. All of these and their strangely harmonious combination with everything that was lovely, and humorous too, in our English countryside filled me with enchantment. I was ambitious enough to try to express something of this in my drawings and make them a record of this, the most wonderful moonlight night in Fantasy. The war put an end to the series of de luxe volumes I have been describing, but during this time I illustrated *Peacock Pie* by Walter de la Mare. The illustration of these lovely poems was a delight for me and made a refreshing interlude in all the war work in which I was soon to be involved.

CHAPTER TWELVE

Pinner

NOW I must write of my domestic life, a phase which I have only scantily described in recent chapters. So my narrative once more recedes to draw together old memories. With them it returns, and is carried yet another stage forward with the tide.

However much we wandered during the week, on Sunday we found a common meeting-place at home. There was a welcome, too, for guests, and many to enjoy it. For my mother, her duties as hostess were matter of conscience. She expressed her kindness in terms of good meals, and there was only one way to respond and that was by consuming them. This our friends were never loath to do. The Sunday mid-day dinner was still my mother's grand achievement of the week. It was a work of art, a symphony in roast beef, baked potatoes and pudding. The first, second, and third movements were so nicely adjusted that they did not detract one from another. This was usually enjoyed by the family alone.

After dinner, those who were engaged to be married departed gloriously in silk hats and frock-coats to meet their fiancées, and to bring them home, where we gathered again for tea. We took this delicate meal in the refined atmosphere of the drawing-room, around which we were seated on the curly-limbed chairs. There was a sweet smell of old rose leaves from a china bowl on the table. If it were summer-time, the french windows would be open, and we could see the little suburban garden with its small patch of lawn. Across this shadows were cast from an old horse-chestnut tree, a relic of the woods that once covered the ground. Between the shadows and along the grass, shafts of sunlight were thrown, reaching here and there to the beds, where they kindled bright flames of red and yellow and orange among the flowers.

The young men who were engaged to be married were resplendent with luxurious growth of hair and heavy but well-trimmed moustaches. They were rather uncomfortable in their high stiff collars and clothes that must not be creased. The girls were charming in high coiffures, blouses with wide leg-of-mutton sleeves, and flounced skirts that rustled on the ground as they walked. After a little polite persuasion, a young lady, with becoming reluctance, would oblige by playing on the piano. Then perhaps the strains of Mendelssohn's Spring Song would float through the room, tempering our gaiety with sentimental thoughts.

The Robinsons were incorrigible singers. You could not stop them when once they got going. In the course of the evening every member of the party either sang or played upon the piano. Many of the songs were old English love songs, such as " Stoop not, Young Lover ", " Drink to me only ", and " Passing By ". Melodies of the day were not forgotten, and " The Song that reached my Heart " and such soul-stirring ditties were sung with much feeling. The programme was varied with more boisterous songs from the Students' Song Book. They were mostly sung by the unengaged, who affected an impatience at all this sentimentality. But it was only a matter of time before even you, Tom, who had held out so bravely, were marked down. You were soon to fall a victim to the epidemic which afflicted not only our family but many of our friends. Where now were the Bohemians we fancied ourselves to be? Where our boasted freedom from the conventions of society? One touch of this complaint and we had willingly accepted the oldest convention of all.

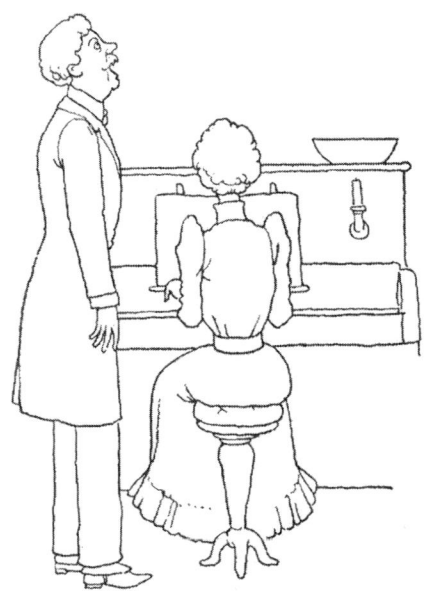

You could not stop them

At this time, the Boer War was gradually drawing to its end. Convinced, as we imagined ourselves to be, of the justice of our cause, we shared the nation's enthusiasm at the beginning of hostilities. We also shared its disappointments at the early disasters, its patriotic joy at the relief of Mafeking and Ladysmith and the dreary boredom of the closing months of the campaign. But we read Rudyard Kipling and found much of glory in these things and they had no serious effect on the peaceful and genial current of our lives.

These halcyon days were brought to an end by the death of my father, in the year 1902, followed a few months later by that of my fiancée's father, John Latey. I remember indistinctly in my early childhood seeing a baby lying all robed in white and surrounded with flowers. My young mother stood by its side, very still. Since then death had not touched us so closely. In our fancied security we had grown accustomed to ignoring it almost as something unreal. When at last we found it in our midst, we were overwhelmed by its dread reality.

I marvel when I count the number of years during which my father held our home together. In all that time he rarely had provision for more than present needs. This position was normal with him, and caused no anxiety as long as immediate expenses were met. Other than his own resources he had little to depend upon except the ravens. Providence, who was our friend, saved us from the necessity of seeking their rather doubtful help. No doubt his life was an adventure, which I am glad to think he enjoyed. He gave expression to this joy in many ways, even in his clothes, of which he was fastidious. Though not ostentatious, they were always as bright as fashion allowed. His modest display of jewellery, of which he was a little proud, was without a hint of vulgarity. I love to recall his humorous philosophy and his patience in face of his opinionated brood. But we were privileged. It was not so easy for others to withstand him.

He might have been more worldly-wise and provident, but he could not have shown greater generosity and charity when these were called for. His old love of the sea never left him. I was with him on a holiday a little while before he died. I can remember him gazing out to sea; for the last time, as we both knew.

Charles was already married, and Tom, after all, submitted to the yoke before me. He married a daughter of the late John Francis Barnett, the composer of a cantata based on *The Ancient Mariner*, "Paradise and the Peri", and many other pieces well known in his day and often played at the present time. Our wedding took place in the year 1903, after a long engagement. I was very busy at the time, and had much work to finish on the day before. In spite of the help of many willing friends, I did not finish work until the small hours. On my wedding morn, I was up betimes, as most bridegrooms are. After a quick breakfast I hurried down to Seven Sisters Road and bought the ring and my rather thin trousseau. Having suitably arrayed my person, I went to the church with my brother George, who supported me as Best Man.

Our wedding needs little description. It was much as other weddings. The bridegroom was punctual, and waiting patiently at the altar rails. He was trying to appear not at all embarrassed, or concerned at the delay of the bride. This, he was encouragingly assured, was not unusual with brides on these occasions. In the quiet expectancy of the church he dared not look round. When at length a stir at the entrance and a rustling of dresses among the congregation announced the bride's arrival, he pretended that it was a matter of no great moment. Unfortunately my preparations had been so hurried that I had not the time to study and memorize the service. However, in spite of one or two errors, which threatened the solemnity of the ceremony, we were duly married.

The triumphal procession down the aisle with my bride on my arm, to the strains of the wedding march; the joyful faces of our friends; the showers of confetti and flowers; the carriages and the jolly coachmen; all these were rather unreal. These things, together with the festivities that followed, the speeches, the wine, the photograph, and the surprising fact that we were married, combined to form a dream-like memory that has not faded from my mind. I can hear the reader saying that this was just an ordinary wedding. It was.

After clamorous God-speeds and farewells, it was all over. We were no longer in the centre of the stage, but two ordinary people on a holiday; or so we wished to appear. A few amused glances at us on our journey seemed to cast a doubt on this pretence. We spent our honeymoon at Bournemouth. It was in the Rhododendron Summer, when Bournemouth, for all its artificial air, has a beauty of its own. The parks and chines were aflame with their colour.

Our first essay at housekeeping was made in a furnished flat. It was at the top of a tall building at the side of a music hall in the north of London. There were no lifts and our home could only be reached by climbing long flights of stone steps. Our evenings were enlivened by occasional bursts of applause which we could hear through the wall separating us from the theatre. When we were entertaining and conversing with friends, the applause would sometimes occur at inopportune moments, and make an unexpected commentary on our conversation. It was disconcerting, for instance, when, in the polite pause following a guest's declining a second helping, a burst of clapping intervened.

We did not suffer these inconveniences for long, and soon moved into more comfortable quarters, where we continued our housekeeping under more satisfactory conditions. We now lived amidst our own furniture in a flat in Cathcart Hill, Junction Road. Our first child, Joan, was born in our

One of the earliest honeymoon trains run by the G.W.R.

Flat life: the spare bedroom

new home in 1904. We awaited this event, not only with a natural anxiety, but as an approaching miracle. Our lives and interests were about to be enlarged. A side of ourselves hitherto unguessed was about to be revealed, and we were going to live in a larger and happier country.

Just before dawn on an early day in June I hurriedly left our flat. I was anxious and flurried as I hastened up the hill to the doctor's. It was a windy and eerie morning, and great clouds were blowing across the lightening sky. The doctor, clad in his dressing-gown, invited me into the consulting-room. After I had explained to him the imminence of the great event, he made no reply, but looked at me very closely.

"Will you take a seat?" he asked.

I did as he requested, and he drew a chair forward and sat down in front of me.

"Have you been feeling quite well lately?" he queried.

"Fairly well," I replied, not quite seeing the necessity for this irrelevant inquisition.

"How's your appetite?" he inquired.

"Very good," I answered quite sincerely.

He then took my hand, and after thoughtfully feeling my pulse for a little while he remarked: "Rather excited, but nothing really wrong. What you want is two or three weeks' complete rest. Why not go down to the seaside for a little while and forget everything?"

I tried to make him understand that I was not the patient, and that I had not called at this early hour on my own account. I anxiously explained to him once more the condition of my wife.

"Oh, my good man, don't you worry about that. Everything is going splendidly, and I'll be round in about half an hour."

The day was breaking and the clouds dispersing when I returned home where I found all well. Soon the doctor arrived, and before long our first child was born on a glorious June morning. After giving all the necessary instructions, the doctor remarked:

"What a lovely day to be born on!" and then quietly disappeared.

At this time I was working in town, one of a colony of artists who occupied the many airy studios under the eaves and in the roof of New Court, Carey Street. I shared one of these with my friend E. Cockburn Reynolds. He was an Eurasian, clever and facile as those of his kind often are. He was a true Oriental, and loved to see our studio gay with coloured draperies and rugs. But he could not bring the bright colours and sunlight of India to New Court, Carey Street. He was frail, and in the end succumbed to the comparative severity of our climate. It was not easy to overcome the racial

The kind-hearted engine driver ("Railway Ribaldry")

difference between us, perhaps we never did, but in our friendship we were fellow-countrymen. He fought a hard fight bravely and gaily, and accepted his doom with the fatalism of the East.

We had now been married about four years, and with our two children, Joan and Oliver, found that we had outgrown our quarters. We were rather tired, too, of flat life in Holloway. Greatly daring, we emigrated to Hatch End, Pinner, in still rural Middlesex. It was an adventure we never regretted. We rented a house where I could work at home. It was amongst a little group of similar villas, surrounded on nearly every side by open country. The garden was a piece of old pasture land, and, as we found, grew beautiful flowers. Most of our neighbours, as amateur gardeners, vied with one another, and we joined in the contest with zest, if not with much success.

In the summer the gardens were full of bloom. There were many horse-chestnut trees. In the spring they set ablaze their glorious candle clusters of white and pink. In the autumn the roads and paths were ankle-deep in their crimson, brown, and yellow litter. The sun shone brightly for us in those days. To have all these things always, and the quiet of the countryside, brought delight and peace after our life in Junction Road. This genial air was not only favourable to the growth of flowers, but to the growth of friendships too, and sturdy plants they have proved. Our next-door neighbours, Ernest Huson and his wife, are near neighbours to-day in London, where we continue a great friendship started over the garden fence at Hatch End.

Our house was in the heart of this little colony, in a cul-de-sac surrounded by trees and gardens. Across the way dwelt Thomas Newman and his small family. He was the manager of a branch of Williams Deacons' Bank, and was later to hold the responsible post of manager of their head branch. It was difficult for me to picture him engaged in banking transactions, though

I believe that he brought a very human understanding to bear on them. He was, I should imagine, of the type of the old-fashioned banker, who was often the family adviser and even the confidant of his client. Thomas Newman's conversation was not often of finance, but rather of books and their authors, of art and artists, of actors, and not least of his garden of which he was fond. He knew many professional men and women, whom I assumed to be his clients. We discussed them and their works, and many serious matters besides, over a cheering glass when I sometimes called on him in the evening.

I can picture him now, returning from town across the fields in the evening; a rather romantic figure. He was slowly walking to some music in his mind, and dangling a bunch of violets, a tribute for his wife. His interesting reminiscences, published under the title *Many Parts*, shows more than I am able to do his many and varied interests. But neither this nor I can show his great courage under almost overwhelming sorrow that has beset him in recent years.

Bert Thomas came to live in Hatch End at this time. We had much in common; growing families, and the precarious means of our profession by which to keep them. But we were young, and it was a good fight in that happy place. He had, and has, a great love of the country and all that belongs to it; old houses, country people and especially young children. We had all of these at Hatch End. He has not wandered as I have since those days. He still lives at Pinner, which, I think, has changed more than he. His sense of humour is just as alive and never mean, and, at its best, has that element of charity which characterizes the work of such humorists as Charles Keene.

Our family is increasing. In 1909, Alan, our second son, was born, and in 1912 the number of our family was increased to four by the arrival of a third son, Quentin. Strangely enough the latter is at the present moment studying the manuscript of this book to find errors in punctuation and grammatical slips. So the blame will not be entirely mine if any should escape his fierce inquest. Children henceforth played a great part in our lives, and in their mother's case, almost the only part. Perhaps it was this that induced me to write and illustrate *Bill the Minder*, upon which I was at work during this time. With their many cousins, who often visited them, we seemed to be always surrounded by children, and occupied by the problems they present. In the love and wonder they inspired there was a fullness of life that is beyond my power to describe. But their mother's devotion, and complete absorption in her task of controlling this lovely and unruly vitality, was most wonderful of all.

Tom was the Columbus who discovered Pinner, at least for me. It is true that as a boy I often wandered as far as Hatch End and Pinner from Edgware. But these early ventures were merely exploratory, such as those of the early Norsemen to North America. Tom's, on the other hand, was made with the intention of taking possession and founding a colony on the banks of the River Pin.

After I had joined him in this praiseworthy undertaking, we often met in the evening at the Queen's Head in Pinner village. This is an ancient inn, and, as I remember it, a place of oak panels and timbered ceilings. In the summer the porch was bright with flowers. Above it swung the signboard, painted by Tom. The landlord, Dawes Billows, was an old C.I.V., very military and energetic. He slapped the counter vigorously as he enlarged on the hard and manly life of the British soldier, and made us feel embarrassingly civilian. For all that, he and his wife were true host and hostess. They had a pride in their house. They took their profession seriously, and it was not merely a matter of serving out refreshments, but continually entertaining their guests as well, a real art of which they had had many years' experience.

Albert Toft, the sculptor, and his wife, often stayed here, and it was a social meeting-place for the village. The little bar in which we met was crowded in the evening, and rather stuffy, but there was room and air enough for our purpose. I even remember the local barber, who had closed his shop for the night, shaving one of his customers at the bar.

But it was best of all on the evening before the fair. I recall one of these occasions. It was growing dark; the roundabouts were nearly erected at each end of the village. The booths and swings were already set up on both sides of the street, all ready for to-morrow. A few children were still at play, but the babies were asleep or being fed by their mothers on the steps of the caravans. Under these some gipsy hands were making their beds. The horses, ponies and donkeys that brought these invaders to the village only a few hours before were resting and feeding in the rich field allotted to them. Here and there a battered coke stove was cooking a savoury supper, the aroma from which mingled in the air with the stale, dusty smell that accompanies these travelling fairs.

The showmen and their wives gathered in the tap-room, where they were welcomed and entertained as old friends from a long journey by Mrs. Billows. They had indeed returned from a long journey round England and Wales. But they were known again, gipsies, fortune-tellers, hoop-la, swing and roundabout proprietors, and the very aristocrats of the travelling showman's world. They now enjoyed a happy interlude in their hard life, and their only anxieties were connected with the weather of to-morrow.

We were often joined by friends from London in our long walks through the beautiful country around us. We once planned a midnight excursion. We took the last train to Chorley Wood and under a full July moon we wandered through the woods. They were mysteriously lovely and silent, except for the weird rattle of some night bird. We had not the luck of Bottom, Snout and Starveling. We saw neither Oberon nor Titania. Nor did we hear Pan playing among the trees. But surely they were abroad that night. We watched for the earliest signs of dawn. There were many false alarms; at last the moon was worsted. Its magic, in which we had walked all night, was dispersed, and the sun rose gloriously over the hills near Denham. When we arrived at this village, it was broad daylight. Thence we trudged wearily homeward under a burning July sun.

Two fellow-artists, P. B. Hickling and S. Jacobs, who will be known as "J" by many students and artists of our generation, accompanied us on this moonlight ramble. They had both been our faithful companions on many a country walk. I do not like to contemplate what we should have done without Jacobs on these occasions. It is unfortunate, but I find it difficult at the right moment to persuade myself that I am without a bump of locality. In over-confidence I would sometimes lead the party astray. But we could always rely on Jacobs to bring us back to the right road. He had a useful prevision as to where we should arrive at critical moments such as lunch-time or tea-time or when it was time to turn back. The expedition was planned accordingly. Perhaps this detracted a little from the spirit of adventure with which we started out, but then we were never stranded for the night in the forest or on the wilderness of the South Downs. We always arrived home for supper.

So many of our friends found pleasure in these walks, that we formed a walking club. It was given the convivial name of "The Frothfinders Federation". It consisted of many artists and their friends. Not to be forgotten among these was our great little friend Philip Pimlott, the perpetual president of the Federation. At his christening his fairy godmother presented him with three gifts. Firstly, she promised that in good time

His Fairy Godmother

he should become a talented etcher. Secondly, he was destined to be one of the best boon companions that any man could wish to meet, and thirdly, he was to be an accomplished step-dancer. I do not think that one could ask for more interesting endowments in a friend.

All the Robinsons—Tom, Charles, George and Will—were of course members. We used to meet at an appointed place near Pinner, early on Saturday afternoon. We would then take a long walk, which we planned to end at some hostelry, usually the Crown at Stanmore. As all the world of those days knew, this house was kept by Mr. and Mrs. Marsh. I suppose that Mr. Marsh would be called a good example of the typical English landlord, a fact of which he seemed well aware. Anyhow, like that rather mythical figure, he was tall, stout, somewhat red in the face, and in manner bluff and hearty. Certainly we were entertained generously, and our sharpened appetites appeased. Everything was on a lavish scale, from the roast beef to the beer. After the meal, we roused Stanmore with our songs and choruses. We would then return to Pinner, still joyfully singing along the country lanes.

There must be something of the pagan in me, for whom these choruses had an almost religious sublimity. I do not think that there is anything which so closely unites a group of people as a chorus. Especially is this so when it is inspired by good ale, beef, vegetables and friendship. For a few minutes you are completely at one with each other. The chorus ends and you are individuals again. But perhaps, as the reader may have observed, I am a sentimental man.

We were young then, and on the whole they were days of happiness. We had troubles enough, but security was so much taken for granted, it was so much the normal background of life that it never occurred to us that it might not last for ever. The rude awakening from this dream was drawing nearer year by year.

CHAPTER THIRTEEN

War

WE usually took a long walk in the country on Bank Holidays; perhaps through Hemel Hempstead, Berkhampstead, and Ashley Green. We come upon the airy village of Hawridge, built along the ridge of the downs. We loiter here by the rectory and the old church built in the middle of an ancient encampment, a relic of wars long since fought out. Leaving Hawridge we wander through the high forest that overlooks Wendover. We do not realize the height we have gained until we approach the end of the trees, when through gradually thinning foliage we see the valley far below. With our backs to the forest there is now revealed to us a wide expanse of peaceful English countryside, bright in the August sunlight, and all the brighter for the gloom of the trees through which we have passed.

We were returning from such a walk on the August bank holiday of 1914. The sun had long since set and we were tired as we tramped towards home along the country lanes.

The mild adventures of our walk and the scenes through which we had been passing banished from our minds for the time being the warlike rumours of the last few days. Before long it was dark, and the sleep of the fields and woods was disturbed by the distant sound of galloping horses. This break in the silence that surrounded us was rather uncanny. As we continued to trudge on, wild conjectures arose to our minds as to what was fast approaching. Presently there overtook us at a rapid pace two fast trotting horses. On one of these was a mounted uniformed orderly who also led the other, probably an officer's remount, by the bridle. They passed us and vanished into the distance. The sound died down and the woods and fields resumed their sleep; but for us, this was the first evidence of the war that was immediately to break out.

To-day it is difficult to imagine how we felt about the war in this August of 1914. Peace in Europe had appeared to be so deeply rooted, it seemed an impossibility that British soldiers should fight on European soil. Not since the Crimea had we sent an expeditionary force to the continent, and to France not since the days of Napoleon. At first we were filled with a wild excitement at the prospect of we knew not what experiences. There was a sense of adventure abroad, even for those who were not going to fight. But underneath all of this was an anger as well as dread which everyone personally felt.

Early in August the war had not seriously broken the routine of our lives. We went to our work, and took our summer holidays as usual. We had planned to have this annual recreation at Seaford. I can remember the delay of our private bus filled with children and luggage on its way to Victoria. The roads were rendered nearly impassable by the troops, cavalry and infantry, and by the crowds of people to see them off; all were in the gayest spirits. It was the departure of the first expeditionary force to France. It was at Seaford we began to understand, though only imperfectly as yet, what war would mean for us. It was here we began slowly to realize the fate of the gallant force that left for France when we were setting out on our holiday. The necessity for more and more soldiers was being proclaimed in the newspapers, and recruiting was proceeding apace at Seaford as at every other town and village in the country. Then there were fears of an invasion, and a powerful light from Newhaven Harbour searched the seas every night, while barbed wire began to appear on the cliffs and downs.

On returning to town and work, I found that already a change was taking place. Publishers were beginning to restrict their enterprise within narrower channels, and these were all connected with the war. There was now no demand for purely artistic productions, for new editions of Shakespeare or other classics, unless they bore some connexion with the all-absorbing topic. Even humour was now taking only one direction. At first I found this difficult to follow and was faced with the possibility of no work. The Moratorium, which was proclaimed by the Government at this time, promised to make things easier for us. However, it was not long before we discovered that this device had two faces, one of which smiled kindly on us while the other frowned. As the war developed, I at last found an opening for my humorous work. The much-advertised frightfulness and efficiency of the German army, and its many terrifying inventions, gave me one of the best opportunities I ever enjoyed.

There was, I believe, a system of propaganda secretly pursued by the enemy to scare the civil population of this country. I can remember some postcards with pictures of nightmare engines of war manned by ferocious Germans. Whence these were circulated it would be impossible to tell. The following incident seems to prove that some of the Germans, at least, thought that their propaganda had met with success. Before the war I carried out a series of drawings entitled *Am Tag*, a prophetic vision of a supposed invasion of these islands by a German Army. This was published at the time when Robert Blatchford was writing, warning the British public of the likelihood of war in the near future. One of the drawings depicted some German spies disguised as birds, trees, stags and other animals. They were closely watching the movements of a little Boy Scout in Highgate Woods.

The button magnets: used by the Germans to render our troops uncomfortable before an attack in force

A reprint of this in a German magazine was sent to me from an unknown correspondent at the front. I quote from the letter that accompanied it.

"I am enclosing herewith one of my souvenirs, which I picked up on my way from Amiens to St. Quentin. . . . This picture I found in some billets in Harbonnières. . . . I don't think Jerry tries to convey to his readers the same meaning as your original idea conveyed. . . . I do believe he thinks that we have all got the wind up.

Apparently "Jerry", who appears to have taken the drawing quite seriously, imagined that it depicted the alarm we were all supposed to be feeling at their frightfulness.

I was now engaged upon a series of drawings mostly published by *The Sketch* and *The Bystander*. These continued until the end of the war. It is interesting to note that the humorous artist's idea of the German soldier at this early stage in the hostilities was mainly derived from old news pictures of the Franco-Prussian War. It was only later that we abandoned these anachronisms. Besides many instances of "Breaches of the Hague Conventions" by the enemy, these drawings contained suggestions to our War Office of methods and inventions to combat those that were directed against us. Although I cannot truthfully state that they were ever acted upon, they were at least received gratefully by the men in the trenches. "The Button Magnet" was considered a representative instance of the enemy's Frightfulness and his disregard of the ordinary decencies of life. It is true that this evil plot does not appear to have been actually carried out, but it was obviously the sort of thing that he would have been guilty of had the thought occurred to him. The same thing may be said of the diabolical device to send 'Flu germs to the British trenches and the inhumanity of "The Tatcho Bomb".

At the same time, the efficiency of the German Military Machine is not denied in these pictures. This is well illustrated in the drawing entitled "Our Special Artist with the War lords at the front", and in the detailed drawing of "The Reconnoitring Mortar".

I was gratified and encouraged by the reception my work met with at the many battle fronts. I had an immense correspondence from all ranks of the army. The letter dated 6th November, 1916, from which I give the following extract was typical of many that I received.

. . .Your "Some Frightful War Pictures" has just reached our mess within the last few days and you can have no idea how much the illustrations are appreciated out here. All members of this mess have been "At it" since the very beginning and your sketches in the various magazines, &c., have always been a source of great amusement to us.

Letters arrived asking my advice as an expert in dealing with the daily troubles and worries of the British soldier. For example I shall quote from an open letter sent to me from the Indian Expeditionary Force, dated 14th May, 1915.

Dear Sir,

. . . Having studied for some time your excellent series of Sketches . . . it has occurred to us that you might be able to offer a suggestion . . . to enable British Officers now serving in Mesopotamia to catch the wily Mesopotamian fly . . . it scorns fly-papers, fly-traps, &c., and attacks the long-suffering British Officer in overwhelming numbers. Any suggestion you care to offer would be received out here with deep gratitude, &c., &c.

My advice was eagerly sought for dealing with all of the plagues that attack the soldier at war—rats, lice, flies, mud and wasps.

I had innumerable suggestions sent to me, some of which I was able to carry out. One of these I developed in the drawing entitled " A Practical Mine Finder ". This was sent to me from somewhere in France. My famous Barb Mortar was suggested by the following, an extract from a letter I received from Belgium in August, 1915.

Seeing a soldier the other day laboriously extracting one by one the barbs from a length of barbed wire I couldn't help thinking that a picture of our Tommies doing this to the Boches wire entanglements would be droll.

At times the suggestion would be quite brief and often from an officer of high rank, in which case there would be added a request that the writer's name should not be published. Such a suggestion was contained in the following brief note.

Dear Mr. Heath Robinson,

Do you want a suggestion for " Breaches of the Hague Conventions "? Try training wasps to sting Highlanders in Flanders.

Yours truly,

Lieut.-Col.

I could not help picturing to myself some dignified senior officer secretly thinking of something very humorous. And then, disguising the fact of his preoccupation with anything so trivial, surreptitiously posting it off to me. However, a drawing embodying this idea was afterwards included in the series.

" A Zeppelin's nasty side slip on a banana skin dropped by a thoughtless airman " was also adopted from a suggestion sent to me from the front—as well as " The American Suction Tank for drawing the enemy from his dugout ".

But these were only a few of the many suggestions I received. This work of

The American Suction Tank for drawing the enemy from his dug-out

mine seemed to provoke a very interesting, and, I think, unusual reaction. Nearly every letter contained one or more ideas for drawings, and often they were illustrated. At the least they were all in the spirit of my work, and this brought me very near to the writers. Without exception the letters were written in great good humour by men who were doing their best to make light of their hard life. No greater testimony could there be than these letters of mine to the brave spirit that was abroad amongst our men in France, Salonica, Mesopotamia or wherever they were stationed.

There were many things at home now demanding my attention. I felt that I had been neglecting scientific research work in connexion with the war. The following letter dated 29th May, 1916, was an opportune reminder:

DEAR SIR,

Please find enclosed herewith photo of jet-testing apparatus which has been named after you by the Royal Aircraft Factory. If you would look in to-morrow or early Wednesday morning you could see this machine working. This machine automatically calibrates petrol jets.

Although, as I have mentioned in an early part of this book, I had had a very rudimentary scientific education, I had never tackled the particular problem of the calibration of petrol jets. I did not realize that petrol jets required treatment of this kind. I had intended giving some time to the study of this, but other matters intervened.

The Zeppelin menace was beginning to haunt us, but the worst form of all enemy Frightfulness was "The Subzeppmarinelin". This fearsome engine of war combined the worst features of the submarine and of the Zeppelins.

There was an unconfirmed rumour that it had been seen off our coast. Whether this was true or false, there is little doubt that the enemy would have constructed such a machine had he been able to do so. We certainly cannot accuse the Germans of want of thoroughness in their Zeppelin campaign, any more than in all of their other warlike activities. Thanks to the vigilance of our secret service I was able to reveal something of the intense training that bomb-droppers underwent in Count Zeppelin's evening classes.

Such at any rate was the humorous spirit in which we tried to regard the very serious position we were all in at that time. I believe that our sense of humour played a greater part than we were always aware of in saving us from despair during those days of trial. The severity of conscription, the shortage of munitions, the terror of the submarine campaign against our shipping and the consequent shortage of food, the rationing and the fear of

The subzeppmarinellin for making sure of your enemy

air raids, were not lessened by the humorist's treatment of them, but perhaps it helped us all to bear them more cheerfully.

For the greater part of the war period we lived at Pinner, though we had now moved nearer to the village. It was here that we had our first experience of raids by aeroplanes, as distinguished from Zeps. In June, 1917, fifteen aeroplanes raided London, killing thirty-one people, ten of whom were children. Sixty-seven people were injured. We could see these raids in the distance from Pinner. But the moonlight raids which soon followed were more visible because of the searchlights and shrapnel.

I had previously seen a Zeppelin raid over London. I was in the densely populated district of Kilburn at the time. We saw high over the City a thin needle-like streak of light as the deadly thing came within range of our searchlights. There was intense excitement amongst the people as the sparks of shrapnel burst around the raider. But it seemed so invulnerable and we so helpless.

I shall quote from a letter of mine dated 30th July, 1917. This letter I sent to a friend and it had gone astray and been returned to me.

We have been having exciting times during this period, which includes the moonlight raids over London. I expect you will be tired with descriptions of these, yet I must add my little. We hear the guns, &c., very plainly from here and see the shrapnel bursting in the sky; and one night, the last of the moonlight raids, we could distinctly hear an enemy machine overhead—they make quite a different noise from that of our machines. Pinner, however, seems quite a safe place; so much so, that we have many refugees here, and the place during the last raids has been full; some even sleeping out in the fields.

During the summer we became a sort of spa or watering-place; many people not caring to go farther afield for their holidays.

I was in London during one of these raids. I was watching the performance of a revue for which I had designed a scene. During the performance the manager announced from the stage that enemy aeroplanes had been reported to be approaching London. They would not reach the city, he said, for some time yet and the programme would proceed. Notice would be given to the audience on the near approach of the enemy. For some time they stood it out bravely, but at last the suspense was too much for them and movements were heard in the galleries. They all began to march out. If I remember rightly, the revue went on to its end, and when I came out into the streets the raid had passed away.

Food shortage and rationing were soon to perplex us, a serious perplexity with a family of young children. We grew accustomed even to this, and to many other restrictions which were drawing closer around us month by month. But the public were still ready to laugh at their misfortunes and difficulties, and I was kept busy.

Towards the end of the war, I was commissioned by an American Syndicate to make a series of humorous drawings of the American Army in France.

For this purpose, permission was obtained from the American army, who sent me an invitation to join them at the Front. After weeks of waiting for the necessary permits and the carrying out of various formalities, I at length found myself entrained at Waterloo Railway Station for Southampton. At the same time a troop train was about to leave. A crowd of relations and friends were gathered on the platform. It was a heartrending sight in spite of the brave cheerfulness of all. The soldiers were to meet the last great advance of the German army in the spring of 1918. The train moved off at last with the men crowded at the carriage windows, with hands waving and voices shouting coo-ee and good-byee. But it was saddest of all to see the crowd dispersing when the train had disappeared in the distance, and the voices had died away.

In good time, I arrived at Southampton. After further formalities and endless official precautions, I embarked on the ship that was to take me to Le Havre. Because of the enemy's submarine warfare, there was no advertised time for departure; we had to be on board at a certain time and wait. It was a beautiful evening at the beginning of May, and the sea was calm. The mails and cargo had long since been taken aboard when at length we started on our journey. All lights were extinguished, and even smoking was forbidden on deck. At first we moved very cautiously down Southampton Water. We passed rows of great ships strangely camouflaged. Some had great dabs of black and blue or red splashed across their sides and funnels, quite ignoring the shape of the vessel. It was as though some mad giant had run amok with a huge paint brush and dabbed about him with freakish intent. It was all very weird in the fading light of the evening.

We continued to crawl along, and now and again the engines would almost stop. After a signal from our masthead, duly answered by little flashes of light away out at sea, we would creep on again. Soon these preliminary manœuvres ceased and the ship increased its speed, putting out all its strength to cross the sea as soon as possible. After a night in the crowded cabin we awakened to find ourselves at the side of a quay in Le Havre.

My first destination was Paris, where I arrived late that night. The city was in darkness, and I was escorted to my hotel by an official from Cooks. It was considered unsafe for travellers to go about unaccompanied after dark, except in the principal streets. To-day it is difficult to imagine Paris as I saw it in the early summer of 1918. The Louvre and other public buildings

American barb trousers
For enabling troops to extricate themselves from wire entanglements

were closed and protected from raids with sandbags. The streets were crowded with soldiers of all nationalities, except those of our enemies. In the Champs Elysées, they congregated on Sunday afternoon. These gardens were then gay with the uniforms and decorations of French and British officers, Zouaves, Indians, Americans, Italians; and the blue-uniformed Poilus were everywhere. Striding amongst the crowd was an old soldier attired in the uniform of 1870. He wore a shako, a dark-blue coat, and wide red trousers gathered together at his ankles.

From the American headquarters in Paris I obtained facilities to visit the Port of St. Nazaire. This was the port through which the greater part of the American army entered France. Although it was taken over almost entirely by the Americans, the French harbour police remained very vigilant. By the time I arrived at St. Nazaire I had a sheaf of forms, permits and visas, both English and American as well as French, and my passport and Carte d'Identité to carry about with me. I became confused when, as was constantly happening,

A more innocent-looking artist it would be difficult to find

I had to produce one or more of these. The difficulty was always to find the right form under the suspicious eyes of the police.

On one occasion, I was making some sketches in the harbour quite openly. I was using one of those large canvas covered sketch books with elastic bands so familiar to art students. It was not at all the kind of book that would be used by a spy, or so I should have thought. A more innocent-looking artist, I am sure, it would be difficult to find. However, I did not appear in the same light to a severe-looking harbour policeman, who presently accosted me. He peremptorily asked to see my papers, but I was taken aback by the injustice and absurdity of the suspicions which I read in his face and manner, and could not reply with the promptness that the situation demanded. I had the usual difficulties and fumbled with my bundle of forms. As luck would have it, I gave him the wrong one and this misfortune seemed to convince him of my guilt.

Apparently, although I had the American and British permits, I had neglected to obtain the French permission to sketch on that particular spot.

The harbour policeman now summoned one of his comrades to his assistance and under this armed escort I was marched off, as they informed me, to the Commandant of the Port. This was all a little terrifying. Visions of at least a night in the local dungeon or even a swift end to all my troubles at dawn floated before me. I was kept waiting outside the Port Commandant's office while the first policeman went in to report his capture. Meanwhile the remaining guard added to my discomfort by suspecting my slightest movement as an attempt to escape. When the first policeman returned, I was taken through various departments and my papers were subjected to a close scrutiny. Finally, I was taken trembling before the Commandant of the Port. Instead of the fierce officer I expected to behold, I was greeted by a most suave gentleman, who was full of profuse apologies which he delivered with Gallic fervour, for all the indignity and inconvenience I had been subjected to. He at once wrote out the permission I had neglected to obtain and I was free. I could not help pretending to continue my sketching under the eyes of Harbour Policeman No. 1.

Full of profuse apologies

Soon after this incident I returned to Paris. On the invitation of the army, I now journeyed down to their battle front in Old Lorraine. Hitherto I had been acting independently but now I was to be more particularly their guest. I met many American authors and artists who held officer's rank in the army. I also met Louis Raemaeker, who like myself enjoyed their hospitality. At that time, the Kaiser had fixed a price on his head. There is little to wonder at in this for those who remember the brilliant way in which the Emperor was satirized in the artist's cartoons. Some little time ago I met Louis Raemaeker at an exhibition of my work. I was glad to notice that the Kaiser had not been called upon to pay up. Only the other day, I was able to refresh my memory of Louis Raemaeker's work. I again recognized a great artist and his genius as a cartoonist. Why have we seen so little of his work since the end of the war? Another interesting personality whom I met was Frazier Hunt, the journalist. There was at the time little fighting in this sector. We were enabled to visit without danger places of interest in the area which was defended by the American army. Toul, Nancy, Luné-

A protected mine-finder sounding for mines

ville, Domremy, Gondreville, and many towns and villages in the neighbourhood of the Vosges. There were shattered houses in the villages, trenches cut across the fields, and other evidences of the enemy who had now been driven far away. My dossier of permits, which were constantly demanded and examined on our journeys, became quite worn and dog-eared by continual handling.

There was one district we visited which had been overrun by the Germans in their first onrush and from which they had later been driven. I remember a wide field marked here and there in seeming haphazard position with clusters of white stones. Here were buried little groups of the defenders where they had fallen resisting the advance of the enemy.

When I returned to Paris on my way home to England, I found that I had outstayed my permission to remain in France. This entailed further formalities and an extended stay in the city. One morning I was awakened in my hotel by a resounding boom which reverberated over the roofs. It seemed to come from some distant part of the city.

Amiability in Paris

In about three minutes' time it sounded again. This was Big Bertha, starting for the second time during the war her plan of alarming the citizens. She certainly failed in this. Although the cannonade went on at three-minute intervals for a large part of the day, I could not see that it made any difference to the Parisians. They pursued the ordinary tenor of their lives as though nothing unusual were happening. I could never discover the extent of the damage caused by Big Bertha. I believe that the shells invariably fell in the outskirts of the city.

I remember with gratitude the manner in which I was always met by those Frenchmen with whom I came in contact. My command of the French language was far from perfect, but they always showed delight in helping me. In a perfectly friendly way they would not disguise their amusement at my efforts to make myself understood. If I entered a little shop, for instance, to make some small purchase, explanations would be necessary. We always thrashed out the difficulties that arose quite amicably, much to our mutual amusement, and, I think, esteem.

I went into a restaurant one morning at lunch-time and seated myself at a long table. All of the seats on either side were occupied with the exception of one upon which I now seated myself. Many of my neighbours at the table were officers in the French army, and they were nearly all decorated with medals and orders. It would seem that French officers wore their medals in the ordinary way instead of only on state occasions. Opposite to me was a severe and pompous officer with a large white moustache fiercely curled. His head was covered with a stiff growth of grey hair like a brush. His chest, well thrust forward, was decorated with many medals. He was talking rapidly and imperiously, between eating and drinking, to a distinguished-looking lady at his side. I was studying the menu which had been handed to me by the waitress. In reply to my queries, which I think she imperfectly understood, she was trying to explain what a certain dish consisted of. We had difficulty in understanding one another. I was about to give in and take my luck when the officer seated opposite to me, who had been viewing me narrowly for the last few minutes, leant across the narrow table and said in perfect cockney English " Fried fish and chips ". Although taken aback, my doubts were set at rest and I ordered " Merlans à la Normande aux pommes frites ".

The enemy's submarine campaign was now at its height. British seamen, rescued from sinking ships on the coast of France or Spain or in the Mediterranean, were often drafted home through Paris. The hotel at which I was staying was frequently full of those men on their passage through France. They usually arrived suddenly, sometimes in the middle of the night, and in the morning I would find many seated sadly in the dining-room. They would soon disappear as silently as they came and a new lot would take their place. It was very tragic, and they all bore signs of the terrible ordeal through which they had passed. My own return to Southampton was not without dread of submarines, though perhaps my fears were hardly justified. The steward informed me that we had been chased by three submarines while I was asleep in my bunk. I am inclined to think, however, that he had an eye on the possible effect this news might have on my generosity.

When the war was over in November of that year, I had once more to adapt my work to changing conditions. Peace, reconstruction and demobilization were among the subjects I treated. I designed a Perfect Peace Pageant. This included ornamental cars allegorically representing various aspects of the peace recently declared. One of the most popular of the series was undoubtedly " The Freedom of the Seas ". Many villages and towns were presented with guns or tanks, captured from the enemy, as souvenirs of the war. Sometimes these were received gratefully, at others with anything but gratitude. Many did not want to have always before them these grim reminders of the agony they had endured. I designed a series of drawings at

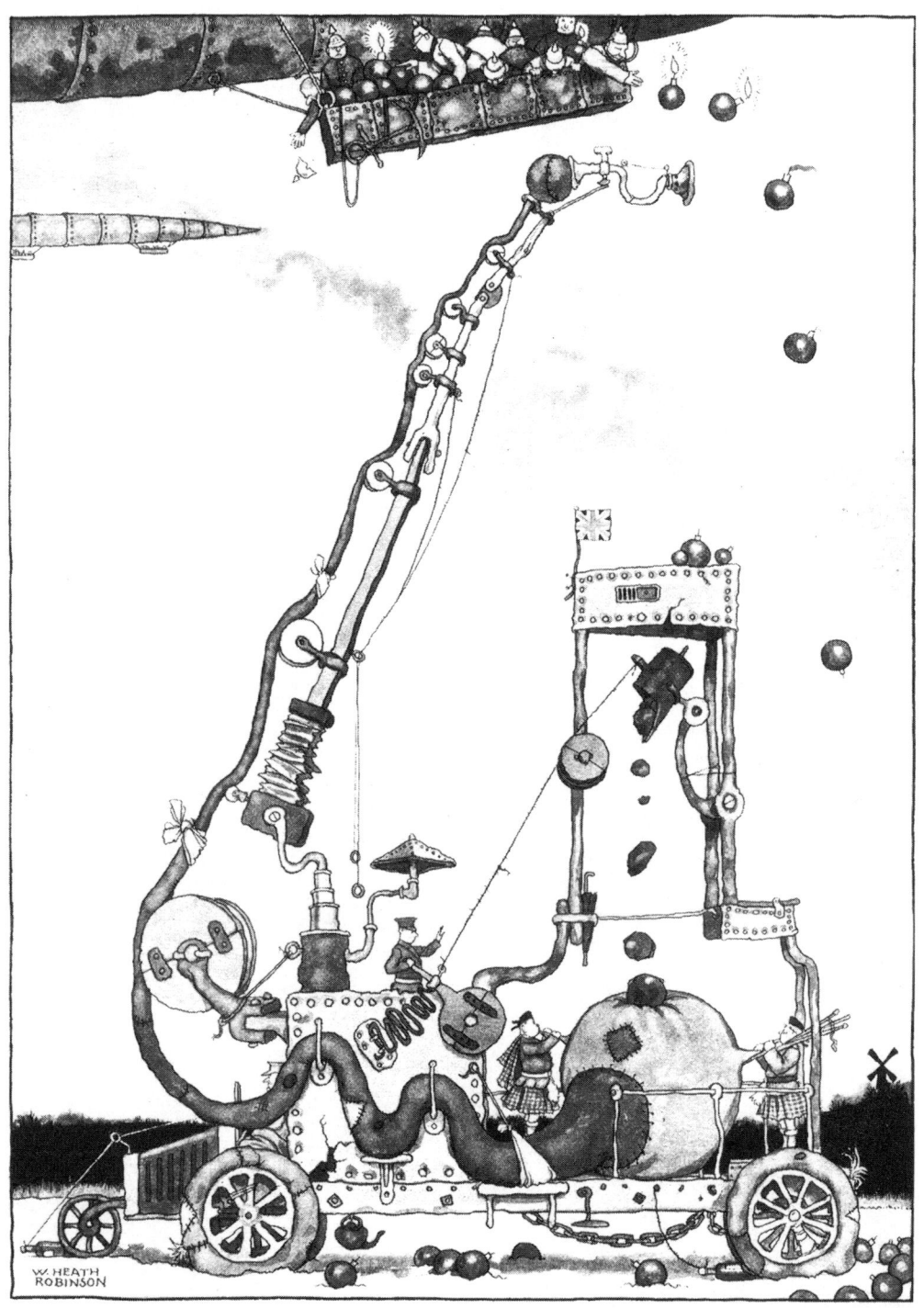

The blow-bomb: an engine for blowing out the fuses of zeppelin bombs

this time to show how these things could be adapted to useful ends. " Using up old Tanks as Motor-buses " was one of these. Reconstruction, especially in the war zones, was a fruitful subject for humorous drawings.

With all of this war-like preoccupation my more serious work was not neglected. As I have already mentioned, it was during the war that I illustrated *Peacock Pie*. Nothing could be more unwarlike than Walter de la Mare's beautiful poems.

On account of the many restrictions we were all compelled to submit to, this last publication was not as elaborately produced as the de luxe editions published before the war. Nevertheless the publishers, Messrs. Constable, may be congratulated for their share in producing this book under such difficult circumstances. Making these drawings was a refreshment during the arid time through which we had been passing. It brought a welcome reminder that there were yet such things as beauty and peace.

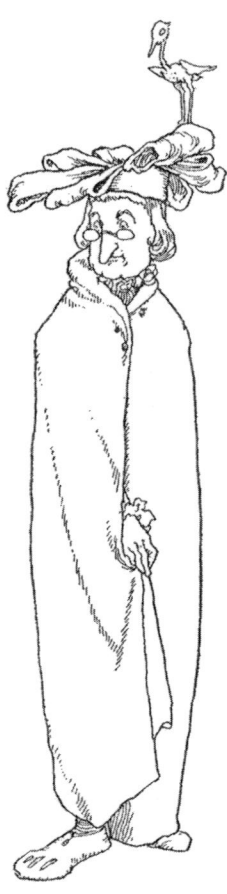

CHAPTER FOURTEEN

In the Country

IN March, 1918, a little while before the end of the war, we migrated to Cranleigh. When we first arrived, there were many German prisoners stationed in an old house near to ours. Every morning they were taken on long farm carts to work in the fields. They would be seated back to back in two long rows. Each had a patch of brightly coloured cloth sewn to his coat to facilitate detection and capture in case of his trying to escape. I do not think there was much likelihood of any making the attempt. They seemed to be very innocent German peasants, who would have been completely lost had they strayed from their guards.

Sometimes they were let out as gardeners to the neighbouring houses. We often employed two of them. They worked well at rough work, of which we always had plenty to do. It is true that our hens appeared to lay a smaller number of eggs, and often only the empty shells, when the prisoners were working for us; but the men looked so simple and guileless that we could not accuse them of any trespass upon our hen roosts. I was instructed not to give the men anything to eat; but, quite accidentally, in the middle of the morning I would leave two mugs of cocoa and

Only the empty shells

some bread and cheese in the garden shed. When I returned later I would find that strangely enough the cocoa and cheese had as accidentally disappeared.

There was one prisoner whom I took to be a German officer transferred by some mistake to this camp of his social inferiors. He seemed to take this error with a very bad grace. He was on one occasion employed in our garden. He arrived in the morning white with an evil rage to which he dared not give vent before me. When he had departed in the evening, I discovered that he had indulged in a little orgy of " Frightfulness " all by himself behind a hedge and had hacked one of my tools to pieces. Whether his unquiet spirit ever found rest I never knew; but I hope that those simple countrymen, his fellow prisoners of war, found happiness and peace when they returned to their native country and families.

However, we came to Cranleigh to banish "Frightfulness" in all its forms from our minds and to lead peaceful country lives. We forgot that we were not country people. But this did not matter very much; we were not out of place. Few of our neighbours could truthfully be called country people. They were mostly retired men and their families—superannuated members of the various services with comfortable pensions, business men and professional men. There were a few artists to leaven the community, which conscientiously we tried to do. Lawson Wood, the well-known humorist, lived at Cranleigh when I first went there. He had a passion for conversions. I do not use this word in a religious sense. He delighted to transform old cottages or farmhouses into beautiful dwellings with lovely gardens. His house at Cranleigh, "Old Tokefield", now owned by Frank Swinnerton, the author, is a fine instance of such a conversion.

Rudgwick is a little village a few miles from Cranleigh. Here lived a great friend of mine, Bertram Prance, with his good wife and children. His clever work in *Punch* will be well remembered. I have a charming landscape of his, a specimen of a side of his work too little known to the public. We are fellow-members of the Savage Club and the London Sketch Club. These good people made it all the harder to leave Cranleigh when the time came. John Eyre, R.I., was another Cranleigh artist. He was a true landscape painter. He had lived the greater part of his life in the open air. This was the kind of life I had so longed to live. He was, I believe, over eighty years of age when I knew him, and yet every morning he would tramp off to the fields carrying his easel and with all his traps strapped about him. There was no feebleness about John Eyre, R.I., and he had the enthusiasm of an art student. I called on him when he was very ill and soon to die; even then he would talk about his art. What great fellows these artists are!

At Cranleigh my friendship with Joseph Longhurst, the landscape painter, began. It was destined to last only three or four years. When I knew him he was an invalid and unable to do much painting. But in his studio were works executed in happier days, which showed the light of genius. Some of our neighbours had beautiful paintings of his on their walls. When he died he left many unwanted canvases. This is so often an added tragedy to the death of an artist. Frequently he leaves behind him the greater part of a life's work to be housed. Unless the artist has a great name, or is likely to have posthumous fame, his pictures are unwanted and valueless. It may be that the work is very thoughtful and conscientious, and an expression, however imperfect, of a high hope and a life's striving, yet at the artist's death it becomes mere lumber.

It would be sacrilege to destroy the pictures, and we have not the wall space on which to hang them. We can only tie them up neatly in bundles and reverently put them away. I know of an artist, celebrated in his day, who died leaving several eight- or ten-foot canvases. If not works of genius, they were at least the result of almost endless care and thought. Finally, one or two of them decorated the staircase of a municipal building in the provinces, but the greater part were turned to the wall.

Old houses, old tiles, crazy pavement, oak beams in a rustic setting were now becoming fashionable. Conversions were not always so excusable and successful as those of Lawson Wood. To convert a small cottage to a large house seemed hardly fair, even when part of the original building jutted out from the side, and the new building was roofed with old tiles taken from an older building. There were more farmhouses than farms, and while the former looked prosperous or even luxurious, few of the fields grew crops, excepting during the war, when many brave attempts were made to revive the fertility of the soil. In some fields the top soil had been removed and sold as loam.

It was, however, a happy make-believe. We could buy antique furniture in the village at reasonable prices. Allowing for the inevitable losses due to time and accident, what a quantity of furniture our ancestors must have possessed.

It would not be fair to suggest that the whole of Cranleigh was affected by this growing craze. Many of the houses were ordinary modern villas and antique effects were not possible: ours was one of these. Others were beautiful and genuinely old houses.

The country has a growing attraction for us all, particularly for those of us who have been bred in cities. First of all, we are compelled to form our ideas of what it is like from books and pictures, and I think we are even influenced by the films. A convention grows up in our minds. At holiday time we gaily venture into the country, hoping to see our ideas realized. The country people, at reasonable rates, are only too ready to help us in this. Between us we manage to get all we came out to see; something that we hardly understand and in which we have little part is turned into the holiday show we were expecting; a more real picture show than the cinema can give us. It is, after all, the artist's attitude, and perhaps the responsibility for this ultimately rests with him. It was he who first went out from the City with his easel and paintbox, and viewed the country curiously as something picturesque and apart from himself.

But we felt that at any rate we were making a bold attempt to get at the heart of the matter. This we only nearly approached in our frequent walks through the fields and woods. We found that spring, summer, autumn and winter are only broad distinctions; that there were more seasons in the country. The process did not cease during the winter, but pursued its course continuously throughout the year. Before one had departed the other was here. It was an unbroken pageant of beautiful changes.

There was the earliest spring when winter is barely over and the first shoots of green appear in the shelter of the hedges. Then there was the spring of the catkins which had an autumn all of its own; and the spring when the floor of the woods is covered with wild anemones and then with primroses and violets; when there are few leaves on the trees to keep the sunlight from their loveliness. This season is soon followed by early summer, the bluebell summer, when the blossom is on the trees. Midsummer is overtaken by St. Martin's summer. Why did St. Martin have a summer all to himself—and the best of the summers too? But each season is the best while it is with us. This season has hardly gone when the varying phases of autumn begin, the last of which has only disappeared a little while when the new growth is making its first efforts against the winter. And so we begin all over again. This rich variety was to be found in everything. There were more kinds of weather in the country than in the town, or so it seemed. Few days were truly alike. Perhaps there was only a subtle difference, but it was usually there for those who had eyes to see, and we were trying to remove the scales from our own.

I admired the heroic efforts of one or two of my neighbours to reconcile the difference between a Town and a Country existence. While strongly tied to town, they tried to live a true countryman's life. They tried, I believe with some success, to combine the life of a farmer with that of a professional or business man in town. Bridge farm was owned by Mr. Emus. It was an old Surrey farmhouse on the banks of a shallow river. It was approached by an ancient bridge that crossed the stream. There had been at this place a farm or settlement of some kind from time immemorial. In the fields by the side of the river prehistoric flint implements were sometimes found. Mr. Emus had a business in town, but managed with the help of his wife and children and some local labour to keep a flourishing farm. I always liked to be asked to tea at Bridge Farm. Mrs. Emus, like a true farmer's wife, knew how to make cakes, and the board was covered with the wholesome results of her skill.

Early in 1919 our youngest son Tom was born. We had now five children. The eldest boy Oliver went to Cranleigh School; our daughter Joan to St. Catherine's at Bramley. The other two boys went to a children's school near by kept by Miss Tapp, a good friend of ours. We were very happy on the whole at Cranleigh, though it was while we were living here that my mother

The new mortar for bridging chasms

died in the year 1921, after a long illness. She was patiently nursed by my sister Mary. My sister had suffered a cruel disappointment earlier in her life and henceforth devoted herself entirely to the care of my mother. Later, with equal devotion, she nursed my other sister Florence who died only a few years ago. She was the wife of Capt. A. L. Garraway who served all through the war in the East. My sister has, I believe, found a great consolation in the work that now occupies almost all of her time. Her writing and illumination are sometimes exquisite.

We soon made many friends in Cranleigh. It is interesting to note the difference in this respect between London and a small community such as ours. In the latter, before long, we knew personally almost everybody. In London you may have the same neighbour for many years and at the end not be on nodding acquaintance with him. To be in such close relationship with so many may have its disadvantages, but I am sure that these are outweighed by its advantages. If there are more opportunities for disagreements, and jealousies, there are still more for friendships, and we had many good friends at Cranleigh. This more human contact was broken for only a few by the morning and evening rush to and from Town. Our domestic concerns and those of our neighbours were never far from us. These, our many friends, our growing family, and the beautiful countryside in which we were living gave scope for a full and happy life such as rarely may be enjoyed in town.

We had many visitors; Alfred Leete whose son was at the school; H. M. Bateman, who would sometimes come over from his house at Reigate; and Bert Thomas, whose eldest son was also at Cranleigh School, would motor down from Pinner with his wife and a bunch of small children all tucked away in a little car. When the car was opened the children would burst forth and greet us with bird-like voices. They would then overrun the house and garden. My three elder sons were now at Cranleigh School. They and our daughter made many school friends who frequently visited us. The cousins from town also paid visits, so that these were exciting times.

One advantage that an artist has over others lies in the fact that he does not belong to any particular class. Class distinctions do not exist for him to the same extent as they do for other people. One day he may be entertained by the squire, and the next evening may find him hob-nobbing in the village inn with the squire's footman. Mind, I do not say that I did this sort of thing, but there was nothing to prevent me. For the artist in a country village, where such distinctions are apt to be rigorously observed, these privileges are more particularly necessary. His right to them was generally admitted and his social vagaries smiled upon by all.

Class distinctions were clearly defined and accepted ungrudgingly by everyone in Cranleigh. On the whole this worked happily. The village itself, dominated at one end by the old grey church and at the other by the school, is built along two sides of a wide Surrey common. It consists mainly of stores and shops that supplied the wants of the neighbourhood and, I have no doubt, made good profit from it. The shopkeepers were a class apart, a position which they occupied contentedly. We saw little of poverty except when the gipsies or tramps passed through the village. We were a detached and self-contained community dropped down into the middle of the Surrey Weald, with little in common with the natives of the district.

A true exquisite

Of these we saw few and they were mostly to be found in the outlying farms. We saw more at the summer fairs and fêtes, when young people, and old people too, from the surrounding villages would come to Cranleigh. Among these could be seen some remarkably fine types of young men and women. It was perhaps a little disappointing for a comic artist who had come out to find old rustic "Hodges" in pleated smocks, but it was good to watch the whole-hearted enjoyment of these visitors to the fair. The best sight of all was to see them dancing on the Green in the evening to the music of the village band.

When we first came to Cranleigh, the war not being over, there were some refugees living in the village and others who sought the quiet of the country during that distracting time. Edmund Dulac was working there, and M. Renée de Boudoir, an artist and writer. The latter was, I understand, a Belgian refugee. I knew little of his work, but he was the most artistic-looking man I have ever met. One day I was doing some rough work in the garden and wheeling a barrow full of clay. I was wearing a suit of old clothes for the purpose. I am afraid that in any case I am not a neat gardener. I approach gardening from a big point of view. My style is without subtlety, and I have not time for its finer aspects. My methods are consequently inclined to be rough, and on this occasion I must confess that much of the clay was distributed about my person. As I was trundling the barrow across the grass in the front garden, an apparition of a beautifully attired young man standing at the gate met my astonished gaze.

He had a rather broad-brimmed black hat and bobbed hair. He wore a grey coat with black velvet collar. The coat was gathered neatly in at the waist and followed gracefully the outline of his figure. His shapely legs were encased in black velvet knee-breeches and stockings. A true exquisite was he and as he drew near he delicately handed to me with daintily gloved hand a little card on which was inscribed, " M. Renée de Boudoir ".

"Will you take this to your master, my good man?" he asked, with a slightly foreign intonation. I bowed politely, and went indoors with the card. I hastily washed my hands and face, put on another coat and returned to greet my visitor. My explanations were viewed with some surprise and a polite urbanity; but I am not sure that at first he was free from a suspicion that he was talking to Mr. W. Heath Robinson's gardener. If this were so, it was soon removed. We exchanged views and indulged in a polite and amiable conversation.

Cranleigh was at least an ideal place for childhood. There was little of the sordid or sorrowful sides of life to be seen. Our children grew apace, but unfortunately our small home did not grow with them. However, I built a large studio in the garden and this relieved the pressure for a time. All of my sons were now at Cranleigh School and we watched their progress and that of our daughter with jealous eyes. Living so near to the school, we knew many of the masters and their families and followed with a personal interest the fortunes of the school. These were guided by the Rev. H. A. Rhodes, M.A., the Headmaster, while the Rev. R. H. C. Mertens, M.A., was Headmaster of the Junior School.

I tried hard to be interested in the sport of the school, perhaps not very successfully; my education in this subject had not received careful supervision. Nevertheless, when I was a boy of about nine years of age I had a sporting triumph upon which I have secretly lived ever since. I was the vice-captain of my eleven, I do not know why. I remember that I was very proud of a large yellow tassel that hung from my cap over my eyes. On one occasion at a match in Finsbury Park, I was put on to bowl. I think I must have been a last hope. We had been trying for the whole of the afternoon to end the innings of a local Bradman.

My over-arm bowling was never my strong point. The ball was liable to take an erratic and dangerous course; so I tried some skilful underhand work. I sent the ball slowly along the wicket; it was hardly in the air for one moment. With what eagerness I watched that ball as it rolled gently through the grass! It crawled past the batsman, in spite of the vicious and misdirected slash he made at it. It then touched a stump with only sufficient impact to dislodge one of the bails. I tried these tactics again and succeeded in taking four wickets in succession and saved the game for my side. The unsportsmanlike way in which our opponents took their defeat was very disappointing. They made no attempt to contain their rage. They called the balls I had bowled

"Sneaks" and me much worse things than that. They showed not the slightest respect for my yellow tassel.

At last, in the year 1929, we were compelled to leave our happy life at Cranleigh and all the good friends we had made there. Our children's schooling was nearly over. Our daughter, who was now a hospital nurse, and our

"Sneaks"

eldest son were already working in London. So, as the others were soon to follow, we returned to the North of London whence we had departed some twenty years before with two little children. It was hard to uproot ourselves from this kindly soil into which we had grown so strongly. This was not the first time we had to start life afresh and gather around us a new circle of friends. Life seemed a succession of these moves. Each brought its own friends, its own interests, joys, and sorrows.

We are fortunate that so many of our friends have survived these changes.

CHAPTER FIFTEEN

The Business Man

WHEN I was living at Cranleigh, I was engaged on many advertisement drawings and book and magazine illustrations, besides lighter drawings for the weeklies. It was here that I illustrated an edition of Perrault's *Fairy Tales* under the title of *Old Time Stories* translated from the French by my friend A. E. Johnson. At the same time, whenever I found opportunities, and fortunately there were many, I indulged my old love of landscape painting. Joseph Longhurst would sometimes accompany me. On one of these expeditions, I had the honour of adding my name to those of many artists in the visitors' list of the world-famous White Horse Inn at Shere. It was an artist's inn and the landlord himself was an artist. The signboard was painted by my friend Longhurst.

I also devoted much time to water-colour painting at home, relying for this very largely upon my imagination. Though it may not be immediately remunerative, I have tried all through my life as an artist to keep this side of my work alive. When I was living in London, the Friday evening meetings at the London Sketch Club were a great inducement to this, but when I moved into the country regular attendance at the Club was no longer possible. This work has played a vital part in my life. With many halts and lapses, it has, I hope, been still progressive. To these financially unrewarded labours I owe more than I can tell.

A little while before I left Cranleigh, I was invited to broadcast at the B.B.C. This was not the first time that I had been asked to do so. The first occasion was many years before in the comparative infancy of broadcasting. On this earlier occasion, I was introduced by *The Bystander*, then under the editorship of A. S. Alberry. At that time the B.B.C. were at home on Savoy Hill. The arrangements were very primitive, though they did not appear so to us. Everything took place in a large room. Many of those who were taking part in the evening's programme were assembled. Everybody was very amiable and seemed to be enjoying the fun as at a social gathering.

When my turn came, I was marched up to a black contraption in the middle of the room, and was instructed to stand before it and deliver my speech into a little orifice. Though at first a little shakily, I believe I did my part satisfactorily. It was all very friendly and the only thing wanting to perfect the sociability of the evening was a few refreshments. But this I understand has always been against the high principles the B.B.C. have set for themselves and so steadfastly maintained. Of course they know their own business, but it seems a pity. In my speech I described my own home-made wireless set. I invited my readers to make drawings of this ingenious machine, and send them into the B.B.C. for competition. There were thousands of entries, and prizes were awarded for the best two or three drawings.

On the second occasion of which I am now writing, the Broadcast again took place at the Savoy Hill. The arrangements were now more efficient. I was seated in a comfortable room before a small table on which was placed the microphone. It was disguised as a kind of money-box—quite a small affair. I was not, as I expected to be, flurried at the thought of the thousands of listeners. I was too much at my ease, and as though I were cosily seated in my own home, to be troubled with such reflections. The only other persons in the room were an announcer and my agent A. E. Johnson. He had given me great help in the preparation of my paper and now acted as prompter. We had agreed upon an elaborate code of signs but fortunately they were not called into use.

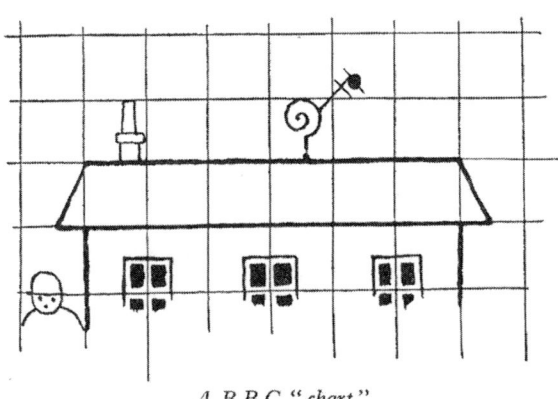

A B.B.C "chart"

Again my paper consisted of a drawing lesson. To prepare the listeners for this, they had been previously advised to take a sheet of paper and rule it into squares. These were all to be numbered. With the aid of this chart, of which I had a copy by my side, I was enabled to guide the listener's hand. In this way I showed them where to draw every line. The subject had to be a simple one, so I chose a Noah's Ark. The listening student was ignorant of what he was drawing until it gradually evolved beneath his hand. One of my difficulties was the dove perched upon the roof of the ark. I overcame this by directing the listener to place a note of interrogation in a certain square and in a contiguous square a crotchet with its tail touching the note of interrogation.

Many of the drawings sent in were clever. Some had been elaborated, making amusing pictures. This broadcasting experiment gave rise to an interesting correspondence. One lady wrote that she was grieved and very disappointed that one who held so high a place in her esteem should descend so low as to make fun of such a subject. I replied that I too was pained that I had wantonly thrown away the treasure of her good regard, but I was puzzled at the same time to know how I had gained it. I made a promise not to use Noah's Ark in the same way again—a promise that I have faithfully kept. More recently still, I was invited to broadcast in the "In Town To-night"

The Man who tried to make a Heath Robinson wireless set

Wireless Enthusiast (to sympathetic neighbour): "Yes, it's quite all right in theory, but somehow or other in practice the darned thing won't work"

programme of the B.B.C. In their present quarters, I found further developments and even greater efficiency.

I was commissioned by *The Daily News* to make a series of strip drawings. I chose as my hero an imaginary character whom I named Mr. Spodnoodle. Actually Mr. Spodnoodle was a reincarnation of Uncle Lubin in modern guise. He was still haunting me and came uninvited down to Cranleigh. He, like all of us, had grown up and become more sophisticated after so many years' experience. He was still trying to move with the times. His adventures were recorded daily for a few months until he died a natural death. Perhaps I should be nearer the truth in describing his eclipse as a fading away for the time being. Like Sherlock Holmes he had an almost uncanny way of turning up unexpectedly to remind me of his existence.

Although these appearances were sometimes provoking, I did not altogether regret them; his mechanical genius was of great value to me in the advertisement drawings I had been engaged upon for some years. Apparently my strange machinery made a strong appeal to manufacturers and engineers. In spite of their absurdity, these inventions of mine were reputed to be mechanically sound. However, I was always invited to study the real machines and processes before my imagination was allowed to play with them. Indeed, this was necessary, as they had to be at least reminiscent of those they burlesqued. This entailed visits to the factories and workshops to make a careful study of the various machines and processes I had to deal with. The more thorough my knowledge the funnier my drawings were likely to be from the point of view of the manufacturers or engineers. It followed also that the humour could only exist for those who had technical knowledge of the subject.

I visited the works of Messrs. Newton, Chambers & Co., Ltd., at Thorncliff near Sheffield. I studied their coke ovens and the methods whereby the valuable by-products are extracted from coal. A ton of coal could be seen taken from the mine at one end of the process, and at the other a tube of shaving cream or a bottle of mouth wash. It was miraculous. I have often thought of suggesting a scheme to them for reversing the process and reconverting the by-products back into coal again in case of over-production.

On behalf of Messrs. G. & T. Earle, Ltd., of Wilmington I examined the manufacture of cement. So far did I penetrate into the mysteries of this, that I was not only prepared to make drawings of the process but to make cement. My designs for the machinery were certainly considered efficient. But as I explained to Messrs. G. & T. Earle, Ltd., I have never wanted to make cement. They were therefore justified in having no fear of my competition. This checked a growing anxiety that I had noticed and put them at their ease at once.

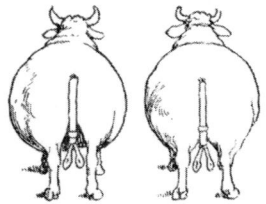

SHEARING DAY AT ONE OF CONNOLLY'S BRACES BULL RANCHES
(*From Connolly Bros.' Booklet*)

The works of John Booth & Sons, structural engineers, of Bolton, were opened to me. I found little to raise a smile in welding, riveting, and the construction of steel frames for buildings. After some hard thinking, I extracted a few laughs even from this unpromising material. As for the currying of leather, I feel that I deserve some kind of diploma for the stimulus I have given to that industry. I think that I am justified in calling myself an expert in leather. For a long time I illustrated a yearly booklet on this subject for Messrs. Connolly Bros., the well-known curriers. I treated leather from every angle and paid many visits to the Connolly currying sheds on the banks of the River Wandle. Wandsworth as everybody knows is situated on this stream. At last I was forced to confess that I had exhausted this prolific subject. I had squeezed out of leather the last drop of fun it was capable of yielding, at least to me.

Another interesting subject that I treated was coal-mining. For this I was invited by Messrs. Fletcher, Burrows & Co., Ltd., to their coal-mines at Atherton in Lancashire. Had I the intention of digging a coal-mine in my garden at Cranleigh I could not have had everything connected with this industry more carefully explained to me. Screening, picking and washing coal, as well as the provisions made for the comfort and convenience of the miners, were all examined. Clad in overalls, I was taken down the shaft of one of the mines.

It was a rather weird experience for one who had never penetrated the earth deeper than the Underground Railway. I put a bold face on the matter and pretended that I was quite at home in this strange situation. In fact there was no reason to feel otherwise in the high, open main galleries. It was when

Removing the wag from the tail
(*From Connolly Bros.' Booklet*)

I was taken through some low and narrow cuttings to the face where they were getting the coal—when I saw the pit props supporting the low ceiling and thought of how much depended upon them—that I felt some disquiet. I do not think that I showed it and hoped that I appeared quite used to this sort of thing. I believe I must have discovered a little concern when I heard a muffled explosion in a distant part of the mine, for I was hastily assured that it was only caused by blasting. I came up from below very black and dusty but otherwise none the worse for my experience.

Steel girders, Swiss rolls, welding, toffee, paper making, marmalade, asbestos cement, beef essence, motor spirit and lager beer were among the many and diverse subjects to be treated. As the principles of mechanics are always the same, this variety did not matter very much.

When first of all confronted with such formidable operations as the rolling out of white-hot steel bars, the manufacture of cement, or the hammering out of steel plates, I despaired of drawing the slightest spark of humour from them. Everything was so efficient and purposeful. Cause and effect were so correctly adjusted that there was no room for accident or mistake which might have been a help to me. All of those engaged in the manipulation of these inexorable forces seemingly ignored anything so trivial as humour by their complete absorption in the tasks they had in hand. But in this I was mistaken. When their stern preoccupation with the work was lifted, these earnest men were like children out of school. Nothing pleased them more than to see that which had held them so tyrannically treated with levity.

These were of the type of men to which I had to appeal. They were men with great knowledge of machines and whose lives were devoted to them. The little that I had been able to learn enabled contact to be made. I had already an audience prepared to be sympathetic; prepared to take an active part in the transaction between us and meet me half-way. This was stimulus and inspiration enough. There always must be this co-operation between the jester and his audience. It takes two at least to make a successful joke. It will be seen from this that for the professional humorist his work is a serious matter.

Many years ago, there was gathered together a society of humorous artists. I think it would have been difficult to find a more serious-looking body of men. In my researches I have never been able to discover who made the first joke, but the humorists are a very ancient institution. They have had many names, most of them a little contemptuous, such as clowns, jesters, Merry Andrews, buffoons, gaillards and witsnappers. There are no entertainers who put themselves so entirely at the mercy of their audience nor whose failure is so tragic.

A patent double-action grinder for mashing asbestos fibre
(*By courtesy of Turners Asbestos Cement Co.*)

In 1930 I was engaged upon the designs for the decoration of the Knickerbocker Bar and the Children's Room in the *Empress of Britain*. These I was commissioned to make through Messrs. Staynes and Jones, the architects. P. A. Staynes was responsible for the decoration of the ship and carried out a large part of it himself—a great achievement. I was honoured to be associated with many famous artists in this work. The designs made for the ship by Sir John Lavery, R.A., Sir Charles Allom, Frank Brangwyn, R.A., the

Whose failure is so tragic

late Maurice Greiffenhagen, R.A., and Edmund Dulac, as well as those of P. A. Staynes are too well known for it to be necessary to describe them.

My designs were painted on large wooden panels in my studio at Highgate. They were then removed to the shipbuilding yards of Messrs. John Brown, near Glasgow, to be fitted into the places allotted to them. I spent three or four days at Clydebank to put the finishing touches to my work. These days were made very interesting for me by the strenuous activities connected with shipbuilding which were continually going on around me. I saw the *Queen Mary* in the early stages of her construction, a long low skeleton lying by the side of one of the banks. Every day I was entertained generously at lunch, which I shared with all the members of the staff and other visitors who happened to be there. This luncheon appeared to be a regular and purely domestic institution of the company. It was a large family party.

The problems that arise in connexion with the decoration of modern ships do not appear to have been solved, though I must confess that I have not seen the *Queen Mary*. There seems to be no precedent to which the designer can turn and he is often compelled to rely upon architectural forms. Yet these seem out of place on a ship. It may be as large as a street, but it is still a ship. There is something absurd in the thought of a marble column or arch in a rough sea. Not all of the designs in the *Empress of Britain* rely upon architectural forms, and many of those that do are at any rate beautiful in themselves.

I had been received with friendliness by everyone with whom I came in contact at Glasgow. But a note of triumph was sounded for me at the close of my visit. I had been previously interviewed by one of the leading newspapers. On the day before my departure it came out with an article on myself and work. A photograph was reproduced and a headline which announced in large letters that

"The Gadget King is Here"

I had the gratifying feeling that the whole of Glasgow and the Clydebank had been anxiously awaiting my appearance; and now that at long last their craving was appeased, they could get on with their work of shipbuilding contentedly.

The year 1934 is memorable to me for the reproduction at the "Ideal Home Exhibition" at Olympia of my ideal home "The Gadgets". Since the days when my "Starting Machine" and the scene of "The Epsom Ups and Downs" were reproduced in the revue at the Alhambra, my work had rarely been so realistically treated. "The Gadgets" might have been the home of the little genius who was never far from me. I was glad that he appeared to be in prosperous circumstances: that he was now settled down and comfortably married. He had a cow in the back garden and a car—not a Rolls or a Morris, but just a car.

His comfortable villa was furnished with many gadgets. He had a bathroom, hot and cold, in which he could be seen through the open window splashing daily. It was not his fault that the visitors in the garden were sometimes splashed. This was only due to a temporary derangement of the hot-water system. What a thriving family of young children he was gathering around him! They were all washed, fed, and put to bed by special contrivances. He and his wife never troubled to use the stairs when they came down to breakfast in the morning. Why should they, when cunning machinery

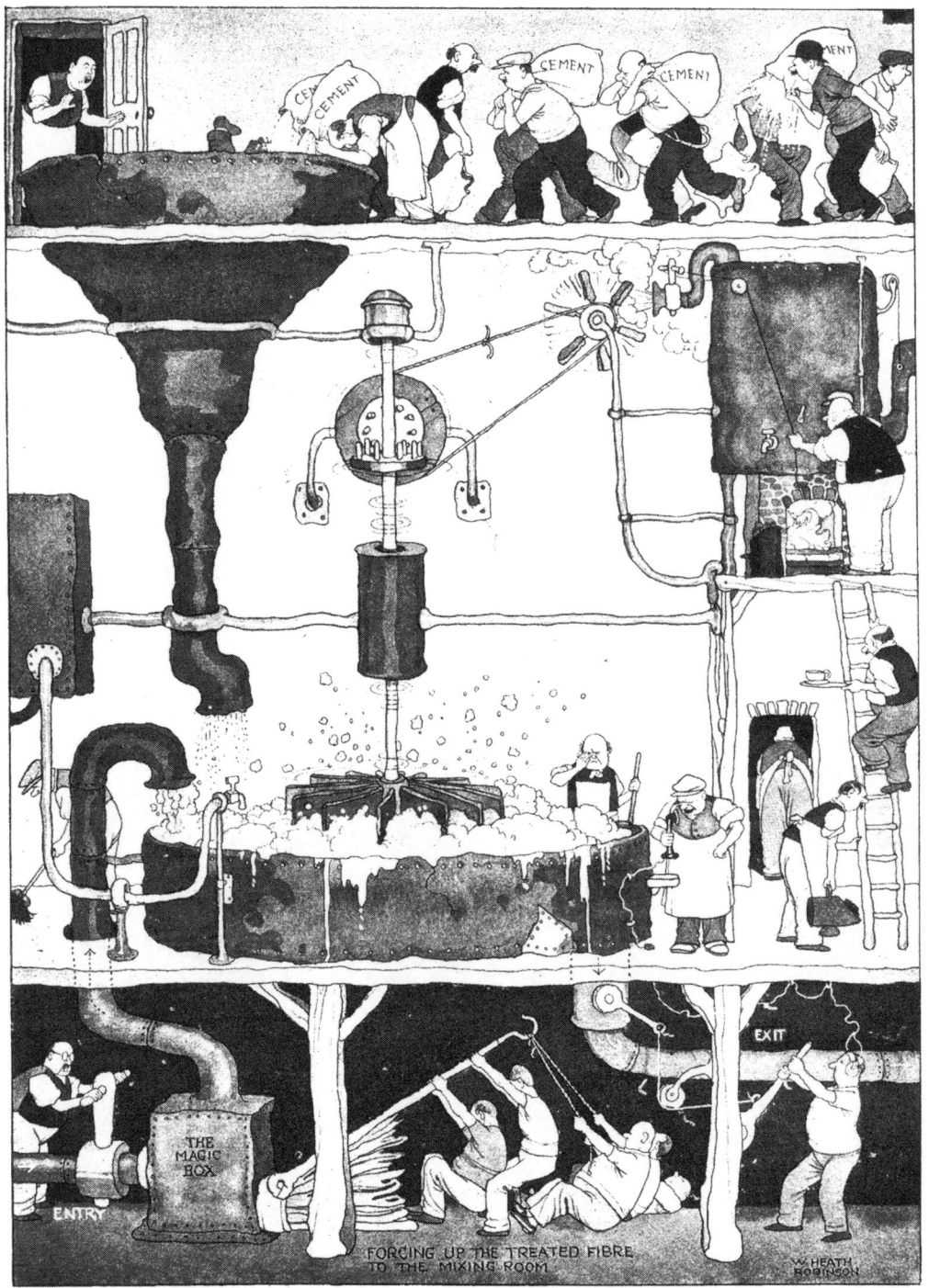

Efficient plant for the successful mixing of treated asbestos fibre with cement

(By courtesy of Turners Asbestos Cement Co.)

was there to let them down gently through the dining-room ceiling to their eggs and bacon below?

"The Gadgets" was a marvel of electrical engineering. It presented problems never found before by an electrical engineer and probably no engineer will be faced with them again. My designs were made without thought of the difficulties involved in realizing them. I did not trouble my head about the matter, and let myself go; yet they were nearly all successfully carried out. Messrs. Venreco Ltd., were responsible for this and for the happy interpretation of the many sketches and designs I made for the house, the figures, the costumes and the innumerable other details of the show. Rarely can a comic artist gauge the effect of his work upon the public. He may see it reproduced in the magazine, but can have little idea of the way in which it is received. He works blindly and thus a great stimulus is missed. This could not be said of my work on "The Gadgets". I had enough of this stimulus in watching the amusement of the crowds of visitors; though I did overhear one earnest visitor condemning it as impracticable.

In the year 1935 the Great Western Railway celebrated its centenary. In their anxiety that the celebrations should really celebrate, the directors, the heads of the publicity department, the stationmasters, engine-drivers, ticket collectors and all engaged in the working of the railway, naturally turned to me. I joyfully collaborated with a series of drawings published under the title "Railway Ribaldry".

In a foreword to this work from which I quote, they state:

> The Great Western Railway celebrates its one hundredth birthday this year, but unlike other Centenarians such as trees and turtles, grows more youthful after a century of existence.

But surely they are too modest and the implied apology was unnecessary? Their mature wisdom wanted no further proof than their selection of one so well equipped for the work, one who had a knowledge of engineering and also of celebrating. The preparation of these drawings necessitated an intensive study of the history of "The Great Western Railway". Besides this, the History of Railway Engineering throughout the country from the days of "Puffing Billy" to the "Cheltenham Flier" had to be exhaustively considered.

My interpretation of the material I accumulated in this way seems to have met with success. The difficulties that confronted me will only be appreciated, when it is remembered that a railway is not merely a matter of railway trains but of stations, signals, waiting-rooms, booking and lost property offices, tunnels and no end of other things as well, most of which

A very early type of Railway Signal now rarely to be seen: From "Railway Ribaldry" (G.W.R.)

were dealt with in *Railway Ribaldry*. The peak of these celebrations was reached when, on a gala excursion, we were all taken in a luxurious train to Bristol. Here we met Sir Robert Horne, J. H. Thomas, the Mayor of Bristol and many other noted people interested in this great occasion.

In the following December I was commissioned to design the back cloth for the Chelsea Arts Club's New Year Ball. This was a fitting close to a busy year and the beginning of a new one.

In the year that followed, the collaboration between Kenneth R. G. Browne and myself began. Our first book *How to Live in a Flat* was followed a year later by *The Perfect Husband*, and we are now preparing an important work on Gardening, entitled *How to make a Garden Grow*. This collaboration seems to have solved a difficulty that I have often found with my lighter drawings. They rarely lend themselves to illustration in the ordinary sense of that term. It is the equal partnership in our mutual productions which is so satisfactory, at least to me. Instead of the finished story being handed to the artist to illustrate, we start level. Before we begin our different parts, we discuss the matter between us. In this way each is able to help the other. A consistency between the writer's and the artist's work is secured which cannot easily be obtained in any other way. My partner in these undertakings has a delightful sense of humour. It is great fun devising with him these little plots to make our readers laugh at themselves and one another.

Kenneth R. G. Browne is the son of the late Gordon Browne, whose excellent work as a book illustrator and magazine illustrator are well known to those of my own generation and of the next generation too. He was the son of Hablot K. Browne, more popularly known as " Phiz ", to whom we are indebted for some of the types by which we recognize the characters created by Charles Dickens.

Such an arrangement as that existing between Kenneth R. G. Browne and myself is only possible with lighter publications. Authors of more serious subjects naturally have their own ideas as to the illustration of their works. The artist must be subject to the writer. He may not have too free a hand and perhaps trump the author's tricks.

But occasions sometimes arise when the illustrator's tendency to enlarge on his subject is excusable and even necessary. He may have to make more illustrations than the subject, taken literally, affords. He may not, as the composer of anthems is at liberty to do, repeat the same phrase over and over again. He may not make more than one illustration to the same passage. In these cases a certain elasticity in his consideration of the story is useful. He is compelled to take the slightest excuse for an illustration. I knew an artist who boasted that he once illustrated the word " The ". I never saw the drawing.

*An artistic way of hiding an unsightly view from a flat
From "How to Live in a Flat" (Hutchinson*

Night duty at one of the first Railway Signals. (G.W.R.)

Building the First Locomotive (G.W.R.)

The well-known classics are the safest books to illustrate. There is no fear of the author's interference. This freedom may be abused, as when an artist illustrates these lines from *The Tempest*:

> Now would I give a thousand furlongs of sea
> for an acre of barren ground

with a full-page drawing of a view on Hampstead Heath which he wished to paint in any case. On the other hand without this perfect freedom of interpretation many beautiful works of art would never have been painted.

I am grateful to the many friends who have readily consented to the reproduction in these pages of some of my work for them.

CHAPTER SIXTEEN

Ordinary People

ALREADY I find myself writing in the present tense. This story of the long journey I have made since 31st May, 1872, is drawing to its close.

On 13th March, 1937, my brother Charles died. It was unbelievable. He was always so alive with an irrepressible vitality, it seemed impossible it could cease. His life had been one of work and some hardship. It had been a brave and successful struggle to be an artist and at the same time to bring up a large family. Yet there was always something of youth and of being on holiday about Charles. I went into his studio a few days before he died. Besides unfinished pictures, there was the incompleted model of a Spanish galleon. It was already taking shape. Painted here and there with brilliant colour it gave promise of the proud and beautiful thing it was to have been. Although unfinished, it was a triumph of the spirit over the years and the many vicissitudes of life that had at last laid him low.

Artists seldom retire

This was at an age when most men retire, but artists seldom retire. Younger men with new ideas and newer ways of looking at things may overtake them and push them aside, but like Charles they go down fighting. I am sure that Tom, the eldest of the three Musketeers, has not given up hope of painting the greatest masterpiece of his life.

Charles inherited his love for making ships from my father, whom he resembled in other ways. He was more concerned with his painting and his ship models than with theories about art. He was an artist first of all and last of all. He had that magic assistance so often given to genius. If he wanted to build a ship, the materials somehow rose to his hands. As with his painting, it was all so easy and instinctive with him.

There was no resisting Charles. His presence could not be ignored in whatever company he happened to be. He was a popular member of the London Sketch Club, where we have all made so many friends. Here you may meet the perennial George Parlby, the stained-glass window designer. Why is it that these artists have been so generously endowed with vitality? I can remember George Parlby in the days of the Yorick Club, some forty years ago, in the days of Sime, of H. D. Lowry and many others. He seemed no younger then than he is to-day. I have known that true humorist and artist John Hassall almost as long, yet he too does not grow old. It was at the London Sketch Club that I first met Reginald Arkell. He was not so well known in those days. But those of us who had read that delightful fantasy called *Columbine*, and the verses with which it was published, knew that here was a real poet.

The greatest masterpiece of his life

I meet these friends again and many other artists at the Savage Club: Bert Thomas; George L. Stampa, whose work on *Punch* everyone knows and enjoys; Tom Purvis, whose fine posters are familiar to all; Ernest Moore, George Belcher, Bertram Prance, Lee Hankey and Albert Toft, the sculptor. His fine head of that almost legendary Savage, old Odell, adorns one of the grand rooms in the new premises of the Club. I do not know how old old Odell

Generously endowed with vitality

was when he died a few years ago, but I understand that this mysterious old Bohemian was one of the oldest men that have lived since the days of Noah. I can remember him as an old man, or so he seemed, performing at a students' smoking concert when I was in the Royal Academy Schools.

The work of Albert Toft is too well known to need comment from me. Particularly his more recent work, such as the bronze bust of Sir Alfred Gilbert bought by the Royal Academy and now permanently in Burlington House, and that of Brangwyn in the Brangwyn Hall at Swansea. Not so well known perhaps to the layman is a book that he has written entitled *Modelling and Sculpture*, which is invaluable to students and a standard work on the technique of the sculptor.

It was at the Savage Club that I met David Low, whose robust and Rabelaisian comments on the times we daily look for, and wonder who will be the next to rub away the smart of his hearty blows. Perhaps he has forgotten our meeting. It was some years since, when the Club was in the Adelphi Terrace. A few months ago one of his cartoons appeared in the *Evening Standard* depicting Harry Tate and myself as ministers in a proposed reshuffle of the Cabinet. I was pleased to be exalted in this way, but I could not help feeling grieved that he had given Harry Tate a position with a larger salary attached to it than I was entitled to in the position allotted to me. I felt justified in pointing this out to Low and received the following letter in reply:

DEAR MR. HEATH ROBINSON,

I appreciate your note about that cartoon. I gave Harry Tate a higher salary because he has a larger moustache.

May I express the pleasure it gives me to find that you are a real person to whom I can express my admiration.

Yours sincerely,
DAVID LOW.

Of course in the light thrown upon the matter by this letter, I was forced to admit the wisdom of his selection. I was glad I wrote.

It was also at the Club that I again met, now as a brother Savage, an old school friend of the Robinsons, Richard Walthew. Then there is that cheerful Savage Percy V. Bradshaw, as well as Kenneth R. G. Browne and my old friend William Latey and many another good friend. It is dismal to contemplate the world without the Savage Club, to picture these great spirits with few opportunities for meeting, wandering aimlessly about the streets. Perhaps they would be reduced to meeting at the cinemas, or in the fine weather to exchanging views while resting on the seats of the Thames Embankment. No, this could not be, the Savage Club is inevitable.

Although not brought so low as this, I have lost some contact with the Clubs by living long in the country. This is a thought full of sorrow for me. I naturally turn for consolation to the life immediately around me. In search

MOUSETRAP.

By courtesy of The Evening Standard

of this I wander around Highgate in the morning. Sometimes my walk takes me along the Archway Road. This is now an avenue of electric standards connected across the road with a network of wires and cables. For part of its length there is a monstrous hoarding covered with posters, elsewhere long rows of houses line the road. Motor-cars, trolley buses, loaded lorries and vans race by continually. A long while ago three boys walked here by green hedges, trees and farms. All that reminds me of the old road are the horse-drawn funerals which still go along to Finchley.

Chat and nod and argue

At other times I stroll into Waterlow Park. There are not many to enjoy its beauty in the morning. A few old retired men meet daily as at a Club and chat and nod and argue. A young man studies the newspaper in search of a job. A lonely and pathetic old lady has brought her breakfast in a paper parcel to eat in the shade of the trees. Soon the nursemaids arrive with their charges, and then a procession of tiny children in blue from the convalescent home near the park. They are led by a nurse with a broad perambulator carrying three even smaller children. All are singing.

It is in the warm light of evening that the park is most beautiful of all. Long shadows are thrown across the tree-ringed valley which falls away from the path in waves of green to the wooded lake below. All over the grass little nests and groups of families are scattered. Where the broadening shadow has not reached them, they are ever moving clusters of almost impossibly brilliant colours. They are so bright that they seem rather to give light than receive it. Above these are hovering toy balloons of rainbow colours. Now and then a ball darts up into the sunlight like a jewel against the trees.

In search of a job

In the distance between the trees the dome of St. Paul's Cathedral and a wide prospect of London is seen in the sunny haze of evening. A procession of people moves along the paths: beautiful young people, happy people, lonely people, old married couples, women worn with kitchen toil or family cares or a life-long fight with circumstance; but all are dressed for Sunday, smiling and enjoying a brief ecstasy as the band plays some sentimental waltz.

Has brought her breakfast

The seats at the side of the paths are nearly all occupied by fathers and mothers. Their children dart to and fro across the paths and right out into the sunlit valley. One child is just a little piece of life clad so lightly in flesh she barely touches the earth as she runs. She only alights now and then. The shadow gradually covers the valley, one last long golden band of sunshine lies across the grass. The colours in this are intensified. They are no longer gay. For a few moments there is even solemnity in their richness and depth; and then they are gone.

The fathers and mothers begin to call their children to them and depart rather sadly for home. They have been at the gates of a paradise which they have only dimly seen. They are again conscious of their burdens. But they are all unconscious that they are bravely supporting the fabric of social life. Without their aid it would fall. They are not original, they are content to be ordinary.

Instinctively they follow the way that has become native to the race, the way whose beginning is lost in the past. Ever persisting uphill and down, at its side may be found beautiful cities, cathedrals, temples, lovely gardens and homes. All that was ever good has passed along their road. On either side is chaos. This road is the line of life of the human race. It travels like a thread of gold across the night, whence, we do not know, nor where it goes; we can but guess.

Journeying along this way, these people are partners in the work of the greatest artists who have lived to proclaim the eternal beauty of the normal life of man.

Even the humorous artist's part in this is not negligible. His humour may be merely refreshing and light-hearted jollity, without which the world would be a sadder place to live in. It may be bitter and contemptuous, or even patronizingly generous, but it can be human and full of charity. This last kind of humour may raise a laugh at the ordinary man, at his foibles and difficulties, but it is a brother's laugh in which he could join. Behind it all is a deep understanding of the vital part he plays and his courage in playing it.

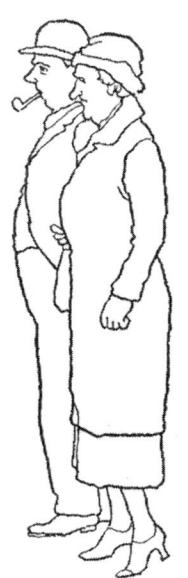

Waterlow Park

We may go to Hampstead Heath on Bank Holiday in jaundiced mood and see nothing but coarseness and wild excess; and hear nothing but raucous sounds as we pass along the high Spaniard's Road. But another mood may sway us, and the coarseness becomes a robust fullness of life, the wild excess a generous overflowing of lovely vitality, all expressing that great human love of being together in crowds and sharing one another's joys. It is as though we had visited some celestial Jack Straw's castle and drained a magic draught; for all is changed.

The Vale of Health tempts us aside. Again, a wide view of London is the background. It is seen through the gaudily painted limbs of a great swing. Like small galleons of barbaric splendour, the creaking swings are manned by jolly crews both fair and brave. They sail nearly to the sky and across the stately vision of St. Paul's and the sunlit city beyond; a whirl of bright dresses, waistcoats, flying locks, and laughing faces. Carried along the road between the booths by the noisy crowd, we no longer see them as a

Yvonne Gregory

W. Heath Robinson
A recent portrait

vulgar mob. They are now a throng of toilworn men and women, boisterous youths and happy children. For one sunny day they are united together to dispel with a great abandon the dullness and cares of everyday life.

Leaving the fair we return along the road, soon to find ourselves members of a large family party. It fills the garden of the Spaniards Inn and overflows into the road. Sitting shoulder touching shoulder on the wooden seats, there is no doubt that we are friends and all know one another. Parting from them at last, we overtake many a little family group walking wearily home.

These ordinary people may not be cultured, they are not much concerned with art. But art, as we understand it, has only been recently invented. Before this word was used as we use it to-day, before it was the self-conscious thing it has become, some of the most beautiful pictures had been painted and stately temples and cathedrals built. On their holidays these people may prefer the Fun Fairs and Big Wheel at Blackpool to the well-preserved fishermen's cottages and farmhouses, with few fishermen or farmers to live in them. They have little understanding of the picturesque and the quaint. But when you turn seawards away from the ugly shacks which litter the shore, when you see these people in all their beauty spread over the yellow sands under a blue sky, a live and ever-changing medley of colours warmed into splendour and harmony by the light of the sun, you own that at times there are few things more beautiful than the ordinary people on holiday.

The story of my line of life now wanders away in many directions. Before I leave it, I must follow one of these that takes a different course from all of them. It ends in a monastery garden in the heart of the Cotswolds. It is restful even to think of it. The monastery is an old Tudor house built of Cotswold stone and roofed with slabs from neighbouring quarries. It was here that our second son Alan retreated in the year 1932, after his unlooked-for conversion to Roman Catholicism. It lies deep in a valley which is surrounded by trees. It is forest country, a country of great trees, giant beeches, and elms. Between these you look down from the road to the grey building below. Dwarfed by the distance, a procession of white-hooded monks can be seen moving along the terrace and disappearing among the trees. A faint smell of incense is drifted on the air. Soon a peal of bells sounds insistently and triumphantly. It reverberates all over the hills and the countryside. It pauses, and a few last sad notes sigh out a requiem to the passing day.

For a little while, one who is not of their church, and who belongs to this jolly laughing world in which we live, envies those who have forsaken it their faith and their great hope.

On the whole it has been a laughing and jolly world for me. I may not have romped with Satyrs in the woods of Arcady, but I have had some pleasant evenings in the Crown at Stanmore. In the light of the lives of Lawrence of Arabia, of Marco Polo, of Sindbad or Robinson Crusoe it must be confessed that my life appears to have been uneventful. But in its narrower sphere it has not been without variety and adventure. I have had hills of difficulty to surmount, though never a view of Mount Everest. Although I have not trodden the Sahara desert, I have had barren places to cross as arid to me. In a low-lying country a haystack may appear as high as a mountain.

Limited as the scope of my story may have been, much remains and must still remain untold. After all it is but the half of a story. The other could only be written by a greater writer than I, by one who could describe the essential and silent part played by a good wife in the life of a man. She is like the prompter who, although self-effacing, directs the play. Without this my story would have been different—and perhaps, who can say? a more foolish one.

But foolish or wise it does not pretend to be more than a plain tale which like all tales must end.

INDEX

Afghanistan, campaigns in, 9.
Alberry, A. S., 171.
Alexandra Palace, 16, 22.
Alhambra Theatre, 114.
Arkell, Reginald, 190.
Aumonier, James, 97.
— William, 97.

Barribal, 125.
Bateman, H. M., 125, 165.
" Bateman's ", Burwash, 126.
Baumer, Lewis, 78.
B.B.C., 171–4.
Beardsley, Aubrey, 91, 120.
Belcher, George, 190.
Bewick, Thomas, 3.
Bill the Minder, 114, 139.
Billinghurst, Percy, 48, 74.
Black, Francis, 87.
Blatchford, Robert, 146.
Booksellers' Row, 32.
Boot, Ernest, 110, 125.
— W. H. J., 110.
— Sydney, 110, 125.
Brighton, 55–6.
— Chain Pier, 56.
British Museum, 75–6.
Browne, Gordon, 181.
— Hablot K. (" Phiz "), 181.
— K. R. G., 181, 191.

Canton, William, 93.
Charlot, André, 114–5.
Coe, William, 73.
Cranleigh, 83, 161–8.
Crosland, T. W. H., 99.

Danes Inn, 59, 91, 92.
Dearmer, Rev. Percy, 122.
De la Bere, 125.
De la Mare, Walter, 129, 157.
Downey, Tom, 125.
Dulac, Edmund, 125, 126, 166, 177.
Du Maurier, George, 3.

East, Alfred, 87.
Empress of Britain, 177.
Epping Forest, 57.
Evans, J. M., 104.
Eyre, John, 162.

Finsbury Park, 17.

Games, Schoolboy, 38–41.
Gilbert, Sir John, 3, 128.
" Good Words ", 3, 93.
Great North Road, 14.
Great War Cartoons, 147–52.
Green, Charles, 3.
Grossmith, George, Jr., 114–5.

Hadley, 14.
Hampstead Heath, 82–7, 91, 185, 194–5.
Hankey, Lee, 190.
Hardy, Dudley, 125.
Hassall, John, 125, 190.
Hawridge, 145.
Heath, George, uncle, 65.
— William, grandfather, 5.
High Barnet, 14, 16.
Highbury, 48, 58.
Highgate, 6, 15, 18, 82, 192.
— Woods, 16, 146.
Holloway, 14, 18, 22, 26, 48, 58.
Holywell St., 32.
Hornsey, 3, 15, 17.

Illustrated London News, 10, 63.
Ingram, Bruce, 110.
Islington School of Art, 71–5.
— High School, 46.

Johnson, A. E., 110, 123, 171.

Keene, Charles, 139.
Kipling, Rudyard, 3, 126–7, 134.

Lane, John, 93, 122.
Latey, John Lash, 63.
— John, Junior, 8, 63, 134.
— William Lash, 63, 191.
Leete, Alfred, 125, 165.
Lelant, Cornwall, 87.
London Journal, The, 3.
— Press Club, 63.
— Sketch Club, 125–6, 162, 190.
Longhurst, Joseph, 162.
Low, David, 191.
Lowry, H. D., 190.

Mahoney, J., 63.

Mertens, Rev. R. H. C., 167.
Montford, P., 78.
Moore, Ernest, 125, 190.
Muswell Hill, 17.

Newman, Thomas, 138.

Odell, 190.

Parlby, George, 125, 190.
Paternoster Row, 94.
Penny Illustrated Paper (The " P.I.P."), 8, 63, 91.
Pinner, 83, 138–40.
Poe, Edgar Allan, 97, 119–20.
Potter, Charles E., 103–4.
Prance, Bertram, 162, 190.
Prater, Ernest, 74.
Purvis, Tom, 190.

Rabelais, 99, 123.
Rackham, Arthur, 126.
Raemaeker, Louis, 154.
Ramsgate, 51–4.
Reynolds, Frank, 125.
Rhodes, Rev. H. A., 167.
Robinson, Charles, uncle, 10.
— Charles, brother, 6, 29, 46, 53, 71, 81, 91, 92, 120, 122–3, 125, 135, 188.
— George, brother, 6, 55, 135.
— Florence, sister, 6, 165.
— Mary, sister, 6, 165.
— T. R., grandfather, 3, 38.
— T. R., father, 5, 6, 8, 9, 134–5.
— T. H., brother, 6, 30, 31, 32, 33, 34, 46, 71, 72, 81, 91–2, 111, 120, 123, 135, 189.
Rouse, W. H. D., 93, 123.
Royal Academy Schools, 75, 77, 95, 190.

Salisbury, Frank O., 78.
Shaw, Byam, 78.
Sheringham, 125.
Shere, 171.
Shorter, Clement, 110.
Sime, 190.
Sims, Charles, 78.
— George R., 111.
Sketch, The, 63, 110, 147.

Smith, Frederick Bernard, 47, 87.
Speed, Harold, 78.
Stampa, G. L., 78, 190.
Stanmore, 142.
Staynes, P. A., 177.
Stephenson, George, 3.
Stroud, Green, 82.
Swinnerton, Frank, 93, 162.

Taylor, Fred, 125.
Temple Bar, 59.
Thomas, Bert, 125, 139, 165, 190.
Toft, Albert, 125, 190.
" *Uncle Lubin* ", 99, 103–4, 111, 114, 123.
Vale of Health, 85, 194.

Walker, Fred, 3.
Walthew, Richard, 47–8, 191.
Waterlow Park, 18, 192.
Wells, H. G., 104, 106.
Wood, Derwent, 78.
— Lawson, 125, 162.
Zulu Wars, 9.